SYMBOLISM

IN LITURGICAL ART

SYMBOLISM IN

LITURGICAL ART

By LeRoy H. Appleton

and Stephen Bridges

Introduction

by Maurice Lavanoux

CHARLES SCRIBNER'S SONS, New York

INTRODUCTION

SYMBOLISM, as it relates to religious art, has too long been of an esoteric nature, reflecting the nineteenth century thinking when symbols were regarded as based on immutable canons of archeological fantasy. Even in the recent past, symbolism has been shrouded in the receding fog of Victorian pomposity which had kept religious art and architecture from developing along normal lines and symbolism from expressing any content of value. Senseless copy and frozen allusions reduced symbolism to a dead parody of that rich imagery to be found in the Old and the New Testaments.

It is ironic to reflect on the paradox that the moment religious art became an archeological pastime the teaching of the Middle Ages—of which the proponents of this archeological pastime claimed direct parentage — was distorted and religious art lost its power to instruct the most humble among the faithful.

Artists and architects have often sought to solve their problems in symbolism through an unimaginative use of fanciful drawings having but a shadowy relationship to the truth to be portrayed. Symbols do not necessarily copy natural objects but express visually a truth for which many words would be required. In the explanation of each symbol illustrated in this book, the authors give us a hint of its meaning and source material for

[v]

further study—enough to lead us to intelligent and visual interpretation of the scriptural texts. They also warn us of certain accepted anachronisms, such as Saint Cecilia's organ and Saint Luke's palette. That is what we can call the sentimental side of symbolism.

Symbolism has sunk to the level of labels devoid of meaning for the faithful to such an extent, that these meaningless labels have been unconsciously accepted by many as being the true visual evidence of scriptural inspiration. This parody has destroyed the impact of symbolism as we see it exemplified in disheartening fashion in the majority of our churches. How far we have come, for example, from the powerful, joyful and even amusing, sculpture of the cathedral at Autun, France! The old masters were not copying slavishly some misunderstood detail; they were carving their vigorous art in the full-bodied acceptance of the wealth of scriptural lore but in the light of their own life. It is this full-bodied acceptance of life that produced such a living and dynamic symbolism that may puzzle and surprise pseudo-traditionalists. But it is that dynamism and robust joy that we need so badly today!

In the realm of religious art we need a new element of vitality, and that can come only through the full exercise of our will and a recognition of our responsibility. Any question of symbolism is a challenge to be met within the disciplines of the liturgy and biblical lore. This book can do much to point the way.

MAURICE LAVANOUX
Secretary, Liturgical Arts Society

January 1, 1959

SYMBOLISM

IN LITURGICAL ART

NOTE
ON THE BIBLICAL CITATIONS

All references to the Bible are made both to the King James, or Authorized, Version, and to the Douai Version. Where the phrasing is identical, only a single citation is given. Where even a minor difference exists, both Versions are cited.

Alpha and Omega   ΑΩ αω

St. John records that Christ Himself said, "I am Alpha and Omega, the beginning and the ending . . . which is, and which was, and which is to come . . ." (King James, *Revelation*, 1, 8. In the Douai Version, *Apocalypse*, 1, 8, ". . . who is, and who was, and who is to come, the Almighty"). References are made in additional passages: King James, *Revelation*, 1, 11 (not in the Douai); King James, *Revelation*, 21, 6; Douai, *Apocalypse*, 22, 13. The same thought was expressed by Isaiah without the use of the vivid imagery: "I am the first, and I am the last; and besides me there is no God" (King James and Douai, *Isaiah*, 44, 6).

Alpha and Omega convey an idea that would be difficult to present by an object from the world of nature, of the One in whom creation began and by whom it will end. The use of this symbol was given impetus by the condemnation of Arianism (the belief that Christ was merely a creature more perfect than other creatures but inferior to the Father, and therefore was not true God) by the Council of Nicea in A.D. 325. The earliest use of the two letters is flanking the Cross, with later use at the end of the fourth century in combination with the Chi Rho symbol (XP). An example of this later use is the decorated halo of Christ in the mosaic in the church of St. Aquilino at Milan. This is thought to have been made about A.D. 350.

A

Anchor

The source of this symbol is St. Paul, "Which hope we have as an anchor of the soul, both sure and steadfast . . ." (King James, *Hebrews*, 6, 19. In the Douai Version, *Hebrews*, 6, 18–19, ". . . hold fast the hope set before us. Which we have as an anchor of the soul, sure and firm . . ."). This is one of the most ancient Christian symbols. It is found in conjunction with the oldest inscriptions in the catacombs as a sign of the fixed hope of Christians. A discipline of secrecy was practiced by the Church during the first centuries to prevent knowledge of the Christian mysteries being learned by unbelievers, and was extended to catechumens who were initiated by degrees in preparation for Baptism. This secrecy gave rise to much early symbolism and inconography. In the present instance the common object of the anchor signified the Cross only to those who knew its meaning.

During the second and third centuries the anchor was combined with epitaphs in the catacombs. In the oldest of these such phrases as *in pace*, *pax tibi* and *pax tecum* appear in connection with the symbol. As a symbolic Cross the anchor was given even greater meaning when flanked by two fishes, the mystic fish signifying Christ and the anchor the Cross. The use of this symbol ended early in the fourth century.

St. Clement of Alexandria (died about A.D. 217) suggested the anchor as a suitable device for rings to be worn by Christians, ". . . if they were to wear them at all, to wear them on the little finger of the left hand where they would be no impediment to labor . . ."

The anchor is also an attribute of the early Pope St.

Clement (about A.D. 91–99) who, according to an
ancient legend perpetuated in the lessons of the Roman
Breviary, was weighted with an anchor and thrown into
the sea. The waters retreated for many years on his
feast day to make his submarine tomb accessible. He is
represented in a twelfth century mosaic in the church of
St. Clement in Rome seated beside St. Peter and holding
an anchor.

Angels

In the earliest centuries the Divine Will was symbolized
by the Hand of God. Angels as instruments of this Will
almost entirely supplanted the Hand in later times.
Although incorporeal, forms were necessarily used in
representing them. These are usually human bodies
with accompanying attributes signifying their functions.
They are a means of communication between God and
men and their mission includes message-bearing,
execution of justice, and worship.

Dionysius the Areopagite in the sixth century com-
piled a systematic treatise on the Celestial Hierarchy.
Although it was primarily theological in purpose it was
influential in shaping the concept of the orders in
Byzantine art. It was introduced into the West by Pope
Gregory (died A.D. 604), was translated by John the
Scot in the ninth century, and was used as an authority
by St. Thomas Aquinas in the thirteenth. This teaching
was set forth at length in a popular form in Jacobus de
Voragine's *Golden Legend* and became the chief source
of reference for medieval artists.

A

A Wings, which are to us the identifying angelic feature, were not used by Christians in pre-Constantinian art. They were too closely associated with favorite subjects in classical art. A staff, as an indication of a messenger on a mission, was the sole attribute of an angel at first. An important early appearance of these creatures is on the chancel arch of St. Mary Major in Rome (about A.D. 440). From that time on they became common as attendants, without historical necessity.

There are three hierarchies of the nine choirs: first, Seraphim, Cherubim, Thrones; second, Dominations, Virtues, Powers; third, Principalities, Archangels, Angels. In the East the manner of representation was influenced by the various grades of court attendants rendering homage to the emperor. The liturgy and mystery plays were the corresponding influences in the West.

The mode of representing the nine choirs has varied constantly from age to age and from country to country, depending upon the interpretation of literary sources. Among the Greeks, the Seraphim have six wings of fiery red and bear a flaming sword; their feet are bare. Cherubim have two blue wings and shod feet. Thrones are depicted as two fiery wheels with four eye-filled wings each. Dominations, Virtues, and Powers, all with two wings, wear long albs, golden girdles, and green stoles. In their right hands they bear the seal of God marked with the abbreviation of the Greek words for Jesus Christ IC XC (sometimes IΣ XΣ), and in their left hands a golden staff surmounted by a Cross. Principalities, Archangels, and Angels appear as soldiers with two wings, golden belts, and lance-headed javelins.

While there is no uniformity in Western depiction of angels, certain features appear frequently and serve to differentiate the choirs.

Seraphim are shown with six red wings covered with eyes. Sometimes they are shown standing in fire or at a later date on a wheel. Cherubim have four blue wings covered with eyes. They hold open books symbolizing their fullness of knowledge and stand on wheels. Thrones are represented with four wings filled with eyes and carrying thrones or scales symbolizing Divine Justice.

Dominations are vested in royal garments, wear crowns, and carry sceptres, swords or books which may be either open or closed. They have two wings. Virtues are vested in copes or dalmatics over albs and hold a chrismatory or pyx. Miracles are attributed to this choir. Powers sometimes hold rods or swords. Their office of subduing evil forces is symbolized by their knightly dress and the demons they lead in chains.

Principalities are dressed in princely robes over armor, with crowns and a sword or sceptre. It is their duty to execute commands. Archangels are shown as warriors in armor or deacons in albs and dalmatics, with individual attributes for identification. From Scripture and apocryphal writings we have the names of seven Archangels: Michael, Gabriel, Raphael, Uriel, Barachiel, Jehudiel, and Sealtiel. Chamuel, Zadkiel, Raguel, Sariel, and Jerahmeel are additional names encountered from time to time. Angels are clothed in ecclesiastical garments such as the alb, with or without a stole, and frequently wearing a diadem with a Cross in the front. A late and charming medieval variation was to show them in clothing made of feathers. Many objects are carried by them, including candles, thuribles, musical instruments, inscribed scrolls, and shields decorated with such devices as the Instruments of the Passion.

Apple

The Latin word *malum* signifies both "an apple" and "evil." This possibility of a play on words may account for the use of an apple as a symbol for the Fall and original sin. In medieval art the Christ Child is sometimes depicted with an apple, recalling the Fall and reflecting the turn of mind which finds expression in the *Exultet* sung on Easter Eve: "O happy fault that merited a Redeemer so holy and so great!" The same thought has a popular manifestation in a fifteenth century carol:

> *Ne had the apple taken been,*
> *The apple taken been,*
> *Ne had never our Lady*
> *A-been heavene queen.*

> *Blessed be the time*
> *That apple taken was.*
> *Therefore we moun singen*
> *Deo Gracias!*

Ark, Noah's

The story of Noah was a popular subject for frescoes and sarcophagi in the earliest centuries of the Church. St. Peter used the ark as a figure of souls saved by the waters

of Baptism: "The ark, . . . wherein few, that is, eight souls were saved by water. The like figure whereunto even baptism doth also now save us . . ." (King James and Douai, 1 *Peter*, 3, 20–21. In the Douai Version, the passage reads, ". . . baptism being of the like form, now saveth you also . . ."). The return of the dove with the olive branch was readily seen as a type of the deliverance of the soul from death. In its earliest form the ark was little more than a box afloat on the water. In medieval times the form of the ark resembled a barn or shed set in the hull of a ship. The raven mentioned in *Genesis*, 8, 6 is a frequent adjunct and is seen feasting on an animal carcass.

St. Gregory the Great saw the ark as a symbol of the Church, pyramidal in form to accommodate beasts and reptiles below, with space above for birds and human beings. In his interpretation, the Church holds the many who are carnal, the spiritual few, and Christ without sin as the apex.

Ark of the Covenant

The Lord gave Moses the directions for the form in which the Ark was to be made (King James and Douai, *Exodus*, 25, 10–22). This chest, overlaid with gold, was surmounted with two cherubim of beaten gold which may have had some resemblance to Egyptian religious images. They were so placed that they faced each other and their spread wings touched. The Ark signified God's presence in the midst of His people, and from it He spoke, giving commands and answers.

The Fathers of the Church saw the Ark of the Covenant as a vivid symbol of the reality of the New Law. St. Thomas Aquinas develops this in great detail: "Christ

A

himself was signified by the Ark. For in the same manner as the Ark was made of satinwood, so also was the body of Christ composed of the most pure human substance. The Ark was entirely overlaid with gold, because Christ was filled with wisdom and charity, which gold symbolizes. In the Ark there was a golden vase: this represents Jesus' most holy soul containing the fullness of sanctity and the godhead, figured by the manna. There was also Aaron's rod to indicate the sacerdotal power of Jesus Christ priest forever. Finally, the stone tables of the Laws were likewise contained in the Ark, to mean that Jesus Christ is the author of the Law."

The Ark is frequently found today in series of symbols depicting the titles of the Blessed Virgin in the Litany of Loreto. *Foederis arca* was first used by Richard of St. Victor (died 1173) as a title of the Blessed Virgin. Although this Litany came into general use toward the end of the sixteenth century, most of the titles, or similar ones, can be found in the writings of the Fathers of the first six centuries.

Arrows

The identifying attribute of St. Sebastian, who is usually represented undergoing the torture of being shot at by archers. Although the arrows were as thick as a "hedgehog's bristles," he survived the ordeal and was later clubbed to death. Arrows are likewise an attribute of St. Edmund, King and Martyr. St. Augustine may sometimes be seen represented holding a heart pierced with an arrow as a symbol of his ardent love of God.

The familiar use of an arrow to indicate direction is not a symbol but a sign. True symbols do not necessarily copy natural objects but express visually a truth for which many words would be required.

Axe

The attribute of both St. Thomas of Canterbury and St. Boniface. In the case of St. Thomas it is the weapon that caused his death, while for St. Boniface it was the tool with which he felled a great oak tree sacred to Thor and thereby gave a death blow to paganism in Germany.

Basin and Ewer

Pilate's ceremonial washing of his hands is sometimes given a place among the Instruments of the Passion. St. Matthew records that Pilate "took water, and washed his hands before the multitude, saying, I am innocent of the blood of this just man " (King James and Douai, *Matthew*, 27, 24). Pilate may have made this gesture in conformity to local custom, since the action is similar to the ceremony prescribed in *Deuteronomy*, 21, 1–9, to signify moral cleanliness in affairs when innocent blood had been shed. The proper placement of this emblem in sequence with the other Instruments will prevent it from being identified with the washing of the Apostles' feet at the Last Supper.

Bat, Fuller's

An attribute of the Apostle St. James the Less (the son of Alpheus), first Bishop of Jerusalem and writer of the

Epistle of St. James. According to ancient legendary sources set forth in the *Golden Legend*, he was beaten to death by a fuller using the club with which he beat out clothes. St. James appears in the thirteenth century sculpture at Chartres with this instrument of his martyrdom. Emblems not necessarily connected with martyrdom were assigned to each of the Apostles during the fourteenth century so that each had something distinctive by the fifteenth century.

Beehive

An attribute of St. Ambrose (A.D. 340–397), patron of beekeepers and bakers of honey bread. The *Golden Legend* recounts that while he lay asleep in his cradle, a swarm of bees descended, entered his mouth as if it were a hive, and then flew away beyond sight. The implication is that of his future eloquence. A similar legend is recounted of Plato.

Book

The representation of books has been used throughout history to signify learning, teaching, and writing. As such, books are shown carried by innumerable saints. Their earliest form was the scroll or roll. Separate leaves bound together (codex) came into use in the fourth century. In the earliest Christian art only the roll was used, and it appeared frequently after the codex came into use because it was familiar and traditional. In a strict sense it is an anachronism to depict Christ with a book.

The four Evangelists were sometimes symbolized in the early centuries by four scrolls or books. These are represented as lying on the shelves of a cupboard in the mosaics of the mausoleum of Galla Placidia at Ravenna. In the mosaics of the Orthodox Baptistery, four altars are used to display the four books. Still another example is in the Baptistery of St. John Lateran in Rome where the books flank a Cross. Books were the earliest and, at first, the sole attribute of the Apostles.

Medieval symbolical thought saw mystery in the closed book, impenetrable secrecy in the sealed book, dissemination of truth by text and doctrine in the open book.

Book and Knife

Attributes of St. Bartholomew who, according to popular tradition, left the Gospel of St. Matthew with his Indian converts and met death by being flayed alive. The flaying knife alone is more often seen in late medieval representations. Among the saints in Michael Angelo's "Last Judgment" in the Sistine Chapel, St. Bartholomew is shown holding the knife in one hand and his skin in the other. The same concept is seen in the statue of this saint by Pierre Legros in the Roman church of St. John Lateran.

Attributes of St. Paul. Early custom gave the Apostles books as attributes. A book was eminently suitable for St. Paul, Apostle to the Gentiles, preacher, and writer; and this he carried alone for centuries. The evidence of

monuments as early as the sixth century which depict St. Paul with a sword is disputed. Definite statements that he was beheaded do not occur before the fourth century, though references to martyrdom are earlier. After the introduction of the sword as a symbol at the end of the tenth century, it was adopted generally, and today the omission of it would be conspicuous.

Quite apart from the historical appropriateness of the sword as signifying martyrdom, it can be understood as a reference to spiritual warfare: ". . . take . . . the sword of the Spirit, which is the word of God" (King James and Douai, *Ephésians*, 6, 17). "For the word of God is quick, and powerful, and sharper than any two-edged sword, piercing even to the dividing asunder of soul and spirit, and of the joints and marrow, and is a discerner of the thoughts and intents of the heart" (King James and Douai, *Hebrews*, 4, 12. In the Douai Version, the passage reads: "For the word of God is living and effectual, and more piercing than any two edged sword; and reaching unto the division of the soul and the spirit, of the joints also and the marrow, and is a discerner of the thoughts and intents of the heart").

"And I saw in the right hand of Him that sat on the throne a book written within and on the back side, sealed with seven seals" (King James, *Revelation*, 5, 1;

Douai, *Apocalypse*, 5, 1). Such a book is also described by Isaiah: "And the vision of all is become unto you as the words of a book that is sealed, which men deliver to one that is learned, saying, Read this, I pray thee: and he saith, I cannot; for it is sealed" (King James and Douai, *Isaiah*, 29, 11. In the Douai Version, ". . . the vision of all shall be unto you as the words of a book that is sealed, which when they shall deliver to one that is learned, they shall say: Read this: and he shall answer: I cannot, for it is sealed"). The seals symbolize the profound secrecy of Divine judgments guarding the eternal mystery.

Bush, Burning

"And the angel of the Lord appeared unto him in a flame of fire out of the midst of a bush; and he looked, and, behold the bush burned with fire, and the bush was not consumed" (King James and Douai, *Exodus*, 3, 2. In the Douai Version, the passage reads, "And the Lord appeared to him in a flame of fire out of the midst of a bush; and he saw that the bush was on fire and was not burnt"). St. Stephen, following the Hebrew tradition, speaks of the "angel of the Lord". "And when forty years were expired, there appeared to him (Moses) in the wilderness of Mount Sinai an angel of the Lord in a flame of fire in a bush" (King James and Douai, *Acts*, 7, 30). The early Fathers of the Church saw the Son of God, the Angel of Great Counsel, in this reference and it later became fixed as a type of the Nativity when Christ came to dwell among men. The burning bush

was used as early as the third century among the subjects decorating the catacombs. Moses is invariably shown untying his sandals. In the *Biblia Pauperum* this episode is linked with the Nativity and doubtless influenced countless representations, for it appears in series of stained glass windows of the medieval period and later. The second "O Antiphon" used during Advent reflects this medieval thought: "O Adonai and Leader of the house of Israel, who appeared to Moses in the fire of the flaming bush and gavest him the law on Sinai; come and redeem us by thy out-stretched arm."

The symbol has also been associated with the Blessed Virgin. An antiphon sung at Vespers on the feast of the Circumcision reads: "In the bush seen by Moses as burning yet unconsumed, we recognize the preservation of thy glorious virginity: O Mother of God . . ."

The Hebrew text identifies the bush as thorn-bush; the Vulgate as a bramble bush. Since thorns are a symbol of sin, the condescension of God to man is seen in the choice of this lowly plant rather than one respected and noble.

Caldron

An infrequently used attribute of St. John the Evangelist derived from a legend at least as old as Tertullian, known to St. Jerome, and still included in the Roman Martyrology (May 6). According to this tradition, St. John was brought from Ephesus to Rome by order of Domitian and by the decree of the Senate was cast into a caldron of boiling oil before the Latin Gate and came forth from the ordeal more hale and hearty than before. This mystical martyrdom (it is an ancient belief that St. John died a natural death at an advanced age) is the justification for the palm of martyrdom he sometimes carries. The incident is commemorated by a chapel near the Latin Gate with the title *San Giovanni in Olio*. Both the caldron and palm signify St. John as an Apostle. His mission as an Evangelist is symbolized by the eagle.

Chalice and Host

The cup of wine and the bread used at the Last Supper have been the symbols of that rite from the time of the catacombs to the present. Both chalice and bread have been represented in the forms familiar in each period as symbols of the Eucharist, Holy Communion, or the Lord's Supper. In most cases, it will be noted that the bread is marked with a cross. As a symbol, the chalice and host (New Dispensation) are often balanced by the Tablets of the Law (Old Testament).

In the thirteenth century the classification of virtues and vices was a popular exercise. An important series of virtues was carved at Notre Dame in Paris which influenced similar ones at Amiens and Chartres. At Paris, Faith carries a shield with a Cross. This is thought to be a late restoration substituted for a chalice. At Chartres, the shield is decorated with a chalice, and Faith holds a Cross in her hand. A Cross rising from the chalice is the attribute at Amiens. Faith in the Middle Ages was founded on the Sacrifice of the Cross and revolved around the mystic renewal of that sacrifice at the altar in the Eucharist.

 Chalice and Serpent

This symbol of St. John the Apostle and Evangelist seems to have been derived from the apocryphal "Acts of St. John" now known only from a few fragments. According to the legend (there are several versions), the Apostle was challenged by the high priest of Diana at Ephesus, whose temple he had destroyed, to drink of a poisoned cup. This he did without harm.

A similar story is told by St. Gregory the Great about St. Benedict, though in his case the vessel broke when he made the sign of the Cross over it, as if a stone had been thrown against it. Old monks may sometimes be seen making the sign of the Cross over a cup of tea or coffee in remembrance of this incident.

CHI RHO. *See* XP.

Christ Child

The Presence of the Christ Child in representations of His mother or St. Joseph is accepted as simple historical representation. In addition to those persons mentioned in the Gospel incidents of Our Lord's infancy, many medieval and later mystics would be unidentifiable members of religious orders if it were not for the Holy Child held by them. Foremost among these is St. Anthony of Padua. While he lived in the house of a Count at Padua, it is told, his host passed his room late at night and noticed a brilliant light escaping around the door. When he looked within through the keyhole he saw the Child Jesus standing on a book St. Anthony had been reading, with his cheek against the saint's.

Other saints who are represented holding the Christ Child are Christopher, Cajetan, Felix of Cantalice, Nicholas of Tolentino, Rose of Lima, and Stanislaus.

Coal of Fire

"Then flew one of the seraphim unto me, having a live

coal in his hand, which he had taken with the tongs from off the altar. And he laid it upon my mouth . . ." (King James and Douai, *Isaiah*, 6, 6–7. In the Douai

Version, the passage reads, "And one of the seraphim flew to me: and in his hand was a live coal, which he had taken with the tongs off the altar. And he touched my mouth . . ."). These words have supplied a ready-made symbol for Isaiah, and he is frequently depicted with a coal held in tongs when he appears with the three other major prophets.

The episode is also recalled in the prayer, *Munda cor meum*, appointed to be said before the Gospel is read or sung in the Mass of the Roman Rite.

Cock

This symbol is often included in series of Passion symbols, recalling the words of Christ to St. Peter: ". . . this night before the cock crow, thou shalt deny me thrice" (King James and Douai, *Matthew*, 26, 34). A bronze cock which stood on a column in the ancient basilica of St. Peter in Rome now surmounts a clock in the sacristy of the new.

In medieval lore, cocks on church towers are like faithful preachers, watchful, and turning to meet the rebellious with threats and arguments. The Venerable Bede observed that the cock is like the souls of the just, waiting for the dawn after the darkness of the world's night.

Crosier

The crooked pastoral staff is a symbol of authority and jurisdiction. The details of its form have been noted as capable of a symbolical interpretation; the end is pointed and sharp to prick and goad the slothful, the staff is straight to signify righteous rule, while the crooked head is designed to draw souls to the ways of God. In accord with this symbolism bishops carry the crook outwards.

The Crosier is probably an outgrowth of the walking stick and had liturgical use as early as the fifth century. Since both bishops and mitred abbots use the Crosier, it occurs too frequently in religious art to be an aid in identification of personages represented. In an early form, the top consisted of a Tau Cross, the arms sometimes formed like snakes. As such it is borne by bishops and abbots of the Eastern Rite.

Cross, Eastern

The upper bar represents the inscription placed on the

Cross at Christ's Crucifixion. The slanting bar in the position of a foot-rest has been interpreted as indicating mercy to the thief crucified on the right of Christ. With additional symbols, this Cross is seen on the dress of Eastern Rite monks. The Cross is elevated on three steps, a skull lies at the base, and the spear and sponge on a staff flank it. Above the Cross are the abbreviations IC (Jesus) XC (Christ) and at the sides NIKA (Victor).

Cross, Egyptian

This Cross with a looped handle appears in hieroglyphics and as a symbolic sign in the hands of the goddess Sekket. Its ancient meaning was "life" or "of the living." In later times, Coptic Christians adopted it as a symbol of the Cross, and this is in accord with the Christian belief that the Cross is the tree of life.

Cross, Greek

This Cross with equal arms came into common use by supplanting XP as a symbol. Although more frequently used in the East than in the West, it was interchangeable with the Latin form in all places until the schism between the East and West. The designation "Greek" is medieval. The more literal Western mind has settled on the form most likely resembling that used at the Crucifixion, while the Greeks have transformed the instrument of cruelty into an ornament.

Cross, Jerusalem

This is equally well known as the Crusaders' Cross. It was derived from the coat of arms of Godfrey of Bouillon, the first ruler of the Latin Kingdom of Jerusalem. The entire device is properly red on white and signifies the five wounds of Christ.

Cross, Jeweled

Frequently called *Crux gemmata*. The Christian regard for the Cross as the tree of life prompted the suggestion of growing branches and flowers. When executed in certain materials, the addition of jewels was a natural development, and the way was open for the Cross to become the symbol of triumph. This was in accord with the attitude of Christians after the edict of Milan in A.D. 313, which gave the Church its liberty. The desire to emphasize the Divinity of Christ rather than His human suffering found expression in the jeweled Cross with the Greek letters A and Ω hanging from the arms.

The Office for the feast of St. Andrew contains a responsory which could not have been conceived by a Christian of the first century: "Hail, O Cross! Thou art hallowed by the body of Christ: His members adorn thee as with pearls."

Cross, Latin

This is the form of the Cross most familiar to the Western world. It is in origin essentially a symbol of Christ, but it has been invested with deeper meanings and by its universal use has come to signify Christianity. The Cross is an attribute of all followers of Christ: "Whosoever will come after me, let him deny himself, and take up his cross, and follow me" (King James and Douai, *Mark*, 8, 34. In the Douai Version, "If any man will follow me, let him, etc."). The twelve Apostles are sometimes symbolized by twelve small Crosses clustered around a large central one. In traditional Christian sacramental practice it is used as both sign and gesture.

The lengthened standard of the Latin Cross may derive from the staff of processional Crosses. It resembles the standard surmounted by a Cross carried by Christ in early carvings. This in turn probably gave rise to the custom of depicting Christ raised on a high Cross in representations of the Crucifixion. It will be found in three forms: as a rough tree trunk with bark, round and smooth, and squared as with a plane. In color it may imitate veined wood, be green to symbolize the tree of life and hope, red to recall the blood of Christ, or gold signifying glory.

Cross, Papal

This Cross with three bars may never have existed for

any real or liturgical purpose. It appears more commonly in North European art than in Italian as an attribute of canonized Popes. Its origin is an artistic

or heraldic development from the patriarchal Cross with two bars. It is not used with the papal coat of arms. In actual practice, both archiepiscopal and papal Crosses are crucifixes borne on a staff.

Cross, Pommée

This Cross with apple-like ends on the bars is assigned to the Archangel Michael in *Harleian MS. 5852* (British Museum). No reason is given.

Cross, St. Andrew's

The saltire form of the Cross has been the distinguishing emblem of St. Andrew since the fourteenth century.

After St. Peter, St. Andrew is the first of the Apostles to be represented with a distinctive attribute. In representations of his crucifixion, he is shown tied to the Cross with cords.

Cross, St. Peter's

A Cross is frequently represented with St. Peter on early sarcophagi. This is thought to be a reference to the words, ". . . when thou shalt be old, thou shalt stretch forth thy hands, and another shall gird thee, and carry ("lead" in the Douai Version) thee whither thou wouldst not. This spake he, signifying by what death he should glorify God" (King James and Douai, *John*, 21, 18–19). There is authority dating from the fourth century for the belief that St. Peter was crucified head downwards at his own request. He is so represented in a tenth century manuscript. While not as common an attribute of St. Peter as the keys, the distinctive position of the Cross when it is used makes identification certain.

Cross, Staff

The Cross carried by St. Philip as an attribute since the fifteenth century generally resembles a ceremonial object rather than an instrument for crucifixion. It is akin to the staves used by St. Michael and St. Margaret in overcoming dragon-like devils. Three explanations are made for the Cross as an attribute of St. Philip: it was his weapon against a dragon (paganism); he died on a Cross; he was a missionary preacher who stressed the Cross as a sign of victory.

Cross, Swastika

This primitive cruciform sign known by its Sanskrit name antedates the introduction of Christianity in both East and West. Its significance was not merely decorative but symbolical in a religious sense. The meanings attached to it are various: resemblance to a tool for kindling fire, hence a symbol of productive power; a symbol of the rotation of the sun; the four points of the compass and its four winds; lightning and the god of the tempest. An analysis of the Sanskrit word reveals meanings of health or life. Ancient examples are found throughout the Orient and also in Palestine, Greece, and Etruria as well as among the Germans and Celts.

Christians rarely used this symbol until early in the third century, when it began to supplant the anchor. This use is an example of a studied intention to reveal the Cross to the initiated while concealing it from others.

Cross, Tau

An Old Testament prefiguration of the Cross is presented in the standard on which Moses raised the brazen serpent. "And Moses made a serpent of brass, and put it upon a pole, and it came to pass, that if a serpent had bitten any man, when he beheld the serpent of brass, he lived" (King James and Douai, *Numbers*, 21, 9. In the Douai Version, "Moses therefore made a brazen serpent, and set it up for a sign: which when they that were bitten looked upon, they were healed"). According to tradition, the mark made by the Israelites with blood on their doorposts was in the form of the *tau* (Greek letter T). This concealed symbol of the Cross is found in the catacombs and has a likeness to the standards used to carry the banners in the Roman army. This symbolism is reflected in the hymn *Vexilla regis* by Fortunatus (about A.D. 530–610). In hymnals of today it appears in translation, "The royal banners forward go, the cross shines forth in mystic glow; . . ."

In a crutch-like form it is an emblem of St. Anthony of Egypt and is worn by the Knights of St. Anthony, who were instituted in 1352.

Crown

When used symbolically, the crown is frequently interchanged with a wreath, and both jeweled metal crowns and wreaths of leaves and flowers are found through all periods of Christian art. This ancient symbol of honor, sovereignty, and victory continued to be used with the traditional meanings as well as the newer Christian implications. There are numerous allusions to the crown in both the Old and New Testaments. (See *Psalms* 8 and 21; also the first Epistle of St. Paul to the Corinthians, 9, 25). The wreaths carved with the inscriptions on catacomb tombs were of leaves. Later, the mosaic workers introduced the idea of the cycle of the seasons by making the wreath of fruit and flowers (wheat, grapes, olives,

and flowers) as in the oratory in the Baptistery of the
Lateran at Rome.

Crown of Thorns

Included among the symbols of the Passion in later
medieval times although it does not figure in early
representations of the Crucifixion. The crown of thorns
was mentioned by three Evangelists, but few writers in
the early church refer to it as if it were still in existence
and venerated. It is certain that what was supposed to be
the crown of thorns was revered in Jerusalem for several
hundred years, from the sixth to the ninth century.
When St. Louis obtained the crown and built Sainte-
Chapelle (completed, A.D. 1248), popular and artistic
imagination prompted its inclusion in representations of
the Crucifixion in the form then known. The relic at that
time was a mere wreath of rushes apparently intended to
tie together the crooked thorn branches (*Zizyphus spina
Christi* or jujube tree). In art, the thorns do not appear
until after A.D. 1300. In series of Passion symbols, three
nails are sometimes intertwined with the crown or it
encircles the letters IHC.

Cup and Staff

Attributes of the Archangel Chamuel whose name
signifies "One Who Sees God." He is believed to have

wrestled with Jacob: "And Jacob called the name of the place Peniel: for I have seen God face to face, and my life is preserved" (King James and Douai, *Genesis*, 32, 30. In the Douai Version, "And Jacob called the name of the place Phanuel, saying: I have seen God face to face, and my soul has been saved"). The same Archangel is believed to have consoled Our Lord during His agony in Gethsemane: "And there appeared an angel unto him from heaven, strengthening him" (King James and Douai, *Luke*, 22, 43).

Dice

Two or three dice are commonly displayed on the seamless robe of Christ in series of Passion symbols. All four Evangelists mention the casting of lots for the garment of Christ. St. Matthew writes: "And they crucified him, and parted his garments, casting lots: that it might be fulfilled which was spoken by the prophet, They parted ("divided" in the Douai Version) my garments among them, and upon my vesture did they cast lots" (King James and Douai, *Matthew*, 27, 35).

Dolphin

This survival from classical mythology appeared in the catacombs and was used as late as the Middle Ages. The swift and friendly dolphin was thought to carry the souls of the blessed to the islands of the dead and was so used in decorative art. Representations of fish precede the use of the dolphin, but in time it became associated in Christian iconography with Jonah and an image of the shrouding, entombment, and Resurrection of Christ. It sometimes appears on a trident as a symbol of the Crucifixion.

Dove

The most widely used symbol of the Holy Spirit. All four Evangelists record the appearance of the Holy Spirit in the form of a dove at the Baptism of Christ: "And Jesus, when he was baptized, went up straightway out of the water: and, lo, the heavens were opened unto him, and he saw the Spirit of God descending like a dove and lighting upon him" (King James and Douai, *Matthew*, 3, 16. In the Douai Version, ". . . and he saw the Spirit of God descending as a dove, and coming upon him"). The words of the other Evangelists are similar (King James and Douai, *Mark*, 1, 10, *Luke*, 3, 22, and *John*, 1, 32). In the earliest examples, the dove is without halo or aureole, but later the cruciform halo

became usual. Prior to the eleventh century the dove was the sole symbol of the Holy Spirit. The dove, combined with or interchangeable with a human figure, became common practice in representations of the Trinity in later centuries.

Seven doves are used to symbolize the seven gifts, and twelve doves the twelve fruits of the Holy Spirit. The gifts are listed in *Isaiah*, 11, 2–3: ". . . the spirit of the Lord shall rest upon him: the spirit of wisdom, and of understanding, the spirit of counsel, and of fortitude, the spirit of knowledge, and of godliness. And he shall be filled with the spirit of the fear of the Lord." The twelve fruits of the Holy Spirit as enumerated in the Douai translation are: ". . . charity, joy, peace, patience, benignity, goodness, longanimity, mildness, faith, modesty, continency, chastity" (*Galatians*, 5, 22–23).

A council of the Russian Church in 1667 felt obliged to comment on the universal custom of representing the Holy Spirit by pointing out that He is in essence not a dove, but God. Pope Benedict XIV in 1745 condemned symbolizing the Spirit in other forms than as the dove seen at the Baptism of Christ.

The dove surrounded with seven flames is made to serve as a symbol of Confirmation by those who must have a tidy symbol for every aspect of Christian life. In the Middle Ages an artist would have depicted the rite of conferring the sacrament.

Doves

The human soul was symbolized by doves in the catacombs, where they are combined with inscriptions or appear in the frescoes of gardens, perched on trees. They are intended as an expression of the Christian soul enjoying paradise. The soul fed by the Eucharist is symbolized by birds pecking at bread or drinking from a cup. The olive branch is a frequent adjunct, as an emblem of peace, and recalls the history of Noah in the ark. The twelve doves on the crucifix in the apse of St. Clement in Rome symbolize the Twelve Apostles.

Dragon

A symbol of Satan, the Devil, and Evil. Listed among the reptiles in bestiaries, it is a composite with characteristics of both the python and crocodile. In its most

frightful form it was described by St. John: ". . . behold a great red dragon, having seven heads . . ." (King James, *Revelation*, 12, 3; Douai Version, *Apocalypse*, 12, 3). Combats with dragons occur in the ancient folklore of the Orient, Egypt, and Greece, and the dragon was usually represented in a common single-headed form.

It has been most frequently depicted as overcome by St. Michael: "And there was war in heaven: Michael and his angels fought against the dragon; and the dragon fought and his angels . . . And the great dragon was cast out, that old serpent, called the Devil, and Satan, which deceiveth the whole world: he was cast out into the earth, and his angels were cast out with him" (King James, *Revelation*, 12, 7–9; Douai Version, *Apocalypse*, 12, 7–9).

The dragon is also used as an attribute of St. George and other missionary saints. In origin the symbol was intended to have implications of the evils of paganism. This gave rise to legends of deliverance from fierce dragons intent upon devouring a whole population, such as that set forth in the life of St. George in the *Golden Legend*.

Eagle

The Venerable Bede repeated the ideas of earlier writers when he commented on the significance of the eagle as a symbol of St. John the Evangelist. "In merit he is likened to the flying eagle in the figure of the four living creatures. For indeed the eagle flieth higher than all birds and is accustomed to thrust his gaze, more keen than that of all living things, into the rays of the sun. And the other Evangelists, as upon the earth, do walk with the Lord, expounding his temporal generation and temporal acts equally and sufficiently but saying little of his divinity; but John, as into heaven flieth with the Lord, and though relating but few of his temporal acts, he knew with loftily soaring mind and clearest sight the eternal power of his divinity, and caused us to know also by his writing."

In pagan mythology the eagle is the king of the birds and an attribute of Jupiter, Zeus, and Odin. In Christian art, in addition to being a symbol of St. John, it is also an emblem of Christ and is found in connection with Baptism, the Ascension, and Last Judgment.

E

Eye

Symbol of the omnipresence and omniscience of God. Usually displayed on a triangle emanating rays, it should be interpreted as a symbol of the Trinity rather than of the Father only. The natural reverence which inhibited depiction of God in human form (the Hand alone sufficed until the twelfth century) explains the popularity of this symbol which appeared late and yet has ample support from Scripture. "The eyes of the Lord are in every place, beholding the evil and the good" (King James and Douai, *Proverbs*, 15, 3. In the Douai Version, "The eyes of the Lord in every place behold the good and the evil"). Its most popular use has been among those of stern persuasions, and it is associated with dreary meeting-houses and long sermons. The Masonic Order has made wide use of this symbol. That such a natural symbol did not come into use earlier than the sixteenth century is surprising.

Although St. Lucy is often represented carrying her eyes on a plate, there is no authority for this in the early accounts of her life. Her death in the first years of the fourth century was by the sword. The eyes which are now a familiar attribute serve as an example of the conversion of a symbolical idea into a fact. Her name in Latin (*Lucia*, from *lux*, light) prompted her invocation by the blind and gave rise to stories that her eyes were gouged out and miraculously restored with an increased beauty.

Fish

A symbol of Christ which had its origin in the acrostic formed by the letters in the Greek word for fish (*Ichthus*).

$$Ιησοῦς = \text{Jesus}$$
$$Χριστός = \text{Christ}$$
$$Θεοῦ = \text{of God}$$
$$Υίος = \text{Son}$$
$$Σωτήρ = \text{Savior}$$

Known as early as the second century, it remained in use until the fifth century. In the catacombs it was frequently inscribed alone, in fishing scenes, and in Eucharistic themes. Clement of Alexandria approved of it as a device for rings worn by Christians. During the years of secret Christianity, it was inevitably popular because of its deep significance to the initiated while it was mere decoration to an outsider. The decline of knowledge of Greek among Christians ended its popularity.

Fisherman

Symbol of Baptism, the fisherman being Christ and the fish representing the faithful. A natural outgrowth of the circumstances of the Apostles' lives and recalling the

words addressed to the fishermen, St. Peter and St. Andrew: ". . . I will make you to become fishers of men" (King James and Douai, *Mark*, 1, 17).

Fisherman's Net

A symbol of the Church: ". . . the kingdom of heaven is like unto a net, that was cast into the sea, and gathered of every kind: Which, when it was full, they drew to shore, and sat down, and gathered the good into vessels, but cast the bad away" (King James and Douai, *Matthew*, 13, 47–48. In the Douai Version this reads: ". . . the kingdom of heaven is like to a net cast into the sea, and gathering together of all kinds of fishes. Which, when it is filled, they drew out, and sitting by the shore, they choose out the good into vessels, but the bad they cast forth").

Fish with Basket of Bread

A Eucharistic symbol used in the catacombs. Seemingly

an allusion to the feeding of the multitude by Christ, its real significance was sacramental. In the most familiar example of this, a glass of red wine is included in the

basket of bread. The inclusion of the fish strengthens the meaning by implication that the food is Christ Himself. This early symbol survived for centuries in scenes of the Last Supper, and the theft of a fish from a platter by Judas was intended to convey his thieving propensities long before the money bag appeared as his sign.

Fleur de lis

The heraldic flower of the Middle Ages, commonly accepted as derived from the lily, is a symbol of the Blessed Virgin. The lily among Christians, like the lotus among Hindus, is the symbol of purity and appears in most representations of the Annunciation. Whether the *fleur de lis* is truly a formalization of a lily or an iris is disputed by heraldists. The origin of this motif has been explained by a reported custom of the ancient Franks of lifting a newly proclaimed king on a shield and placing an iris in his hand as a sceptre. Whatever its origin, the *fleur de lis* by long use and common acceptance is a lily and is associated with the Virgin.

Fountain

Symbol of the Virgin. Late medieval devotion added many poetical images to the prayers addressed to Our Lady. Commentators on the Song of Solomon (called

the Canticle of Canticles in the Douai Version) attributed certain phrases to her, and these found visual expression as symbols: ". . . my spouse; a spring shut up, a fountain sealed" (King James, *Song of Solomon*, 4, 12. In the Douai Version, *Canticle of Canticles*, 4, 12, ". . . my spouse, is a garden enclosed, . . . a fountain sealed up").

Garden, Enclosed

A symbol of the Virgin based on a phrase from the Song of Solomon, "A garden inclosed is my sister, . . ." (King James, *Song of Solomon*, 4, 12. In the Douai Version, *Canticle of Canticles*, 4, 12, "My sister, . . . is a garden enclosed . . ."). St. Ambrose, commenting on this verse in *De Virginibus*, wrote, "Only in a garden upon which, by such a sealing, God's image has been impressed, can the well-spring of the heart shine forth in pure waves . . . There virtue is fenced round with the lofty hedge of spiritual walls, and hides itself from all robbers. Even as a garden enclosed against thieves is green with vines, smells of olives, and shines with roses, so in the garden of holy virginity there grow, smell, and shine the vines of piety, the olives of peace and the red roses of chastity."

Gate of Heaven

A symbol of the Virgin developed from one of the titles

included in the Litany of Loreto, it is justified by the belief that she was the gate whereby Christ came to open Heaven to men. The first use of the title is attributed to St. Peter Damian in the eleventh century. Similar expressions are found in the *Alma Redemptoris* of the eleventh century and *Ave Regina Coelorum* of the fourteenth century.

Grapes

In combination with wheat, grapes are a readily recognized symbol of the Holy Eucharist. The popularity and frequent use of this symbol, which in its emphasis on the unity resultant from the parts combined in the species is in accord with deep Christian concepts, has tended to give it a triviality in execution by artists and designers.

Gridiron

Attribute of St. Lawrence who was martyred A.D. 258 by being roasted alive.

Halberd

An attribute of St. Matthias derived from legends of his martyrdom. This is variable in form, and both scimitar and sword are also used.

Hand

This was the symbol constantly in use during the first eleven centuries to express the Presence and Will of God the Father. It was usually shown emerging from a cloud which concealed the Majesty no man can behold and live. As such it continued in use until the seventeenth century, although a head began to appear in the twelfth. There are many variations in position: open, with or without rays, to suggest beneficence; blessing, in both the Latin manner (two forefingers extended) and the Eastern (the middle finger bent with the thumb crossed upon the fourth finger).

Small human figures are sometimes held in a hand of monumental scale to signify the souls of the righteous. "But the souls of the just are in the hand of God: and the torment of death shall not touch them" (Douai, *Wisdom*, 3, 1. The Apocrypha in the King James Version reads approximately the same).

Hat, Red

The chief badge of a cardinal and an anachronistic attribute of St. Jerome who was certainly not a cardinal. Its use may have been prompted by the fact that he was secretary to Pope Damasus I. The use of a cardinal's regalia for St. Jerome began toward the end of the thirteenth century. In early representations, the tassels on the hat vary in number but are now fixed at fifteen to a side when displayed.

Heart

Symbol of charity. The systematizing of thought on morals in the late Middle Ages guided artists in their grouping of the virtues and in devising appropriate symbols for them. Frequently figures were used, and Charity gave food to children, holding a heart aloft at the same time. At the present day, the heart is practically the sole symbol recognized or used for Charity.

A flaming heart is an attribute of St. Augustine of Hippo. A heart inscribed with IHS or pierced with an arrow is appropriate to St. Teresa of Avila.

Heart, Sacred

Symbol of the love of Christ, popular as early as the thirteenth century, when it was displayed heraldically with the wounded hands and feet of Our Lord. Great impetus was given to the use of this symbol by St. Margaret Mary Alacoque (A.D. 1647–1690). In the Roman Catholic Church, the image of the Sacred Heart in public places must combine the Heart with the figure of Christ. It is customarily surrounded with the Crown of Thorns, enveloped with flames, and surmounted with a Cross.

House of Gold

A symbol of Our Lady derived from an invocation in the Litany of Loreto. Cardinal Isidore of Thessalonica is credited with having first used the phrase, A.D. 1463.

IC, XC, IHC, XPC

Monograms which are composed of the first and last (IC, XC), or the first, second and last (IHC, XPC)

IC XC IHC XPC

IC XC
NI KA

letters of the Greek words "Jesus" and "Christ" (IHCOϒC XPICTOC). In traditional Byzantine painting, the figure of Christ is invariably identified by the use of one or other of these abbreviations. The Cross is sometimes flanked with them and with the added word NIKA (NIKH).

IHS, IHC

IHC IHS

The first three, or the first two and last, letters of the name "Jesus" in Greek. The letter *sigma* (C in cursive script; Σ in print) of the Greek alphabet becomes "S" in the Latin alphabet; the horizontal bar sign which indicated an abbreviation developed into a Latin Cross. With these changes, a decline in the knowledge of Greek, and a widespread use of the symbolical device in monogrammatic form, other meanings were attributed to it. St. Bernardine of Siena (A.D. 1380–1444) is credited with having made the interpretation of "Jesus Hominum Salvator" (Jesus, Savior of Men) popular. Other popular misconceptions of its meaning (readily understandable when written I.H.S.) are "In hoc signo (vinces)," "I have suffered," or "Jesus, Heiland, Seligmacher." Stafford in *Christian Symbolism in the Evangelical Churches* reports that this device embroidered on an altar cloth was mistaken for the initials of the devout woman who had done the work. It would be wise if its use were confined to those places where the full form of the Holy Name would be appropriate.

I.N.R.I.

An abbreviation using the initials only (properly separated by periods) of the Latin words inscribed as a title on the Cross of Christ. The Latin words in full are *Iesus Nazarenus Rex Iudaeorum*. This is described by St. John in his Gospel: ". . . Pilate wrote a title, and put it on the cross. And the writing was, Jesus of Nazareth the King of the Jews . . . and it was written in Hebrew, and Greek, and Latin" (King James and Douai, *John*, 19, 19–20).

The custom of using the initial letters only is found in Italian art of the thirteenth century. Prior to that time the title was either inscribed in full or omitted.

 Ichthus (*Ιχθύς*)

The Greek word for fish whose letters constitute an acrostic for the phrase "Jesus Christ Son of God and Savior." *See* Fish.

Instruments of the Passion

The heraldic development of the coat of arms of Christ is as old as the fourteenth century. The common practice was to group some of the instruments around the Cross on a shield. A variation on this is a stone

carving at Wells Cathedral where the instruments are displayed as ornamentation on the letters IHC. In the fifteenth century the emblems were treated as charges on shields in series extending to as many as twenty-four, as at Great Malvern Priory Church in Worcestershire. Such a series, following the account of the Passion recorded in the Gospels, would include the following: Thirty Pieces of Silver, Lantern, Club and Reed-mace, Kiss of Judas, Blindfolding of Jesus, Hand striking Jesus, Bystanders spitting on Jesus, Cock, IHC, Crown of Thorns, Reed Sceptre, Purple Robe, Column of the Scourging, Scourges, Basin and Ewer, Vernicle, Vestigia Salvatoris, Lance or Spear and Reed with Sponge, Nails and Hammer, Coat and Dice, Five Wounds, Vat of Vinegar, Pincers, Ladder, Sepulchre with Christ of Pity.

In both Spanish and Northern art the symbols became important adjuncts to representations of the Mass of St. Gregory in the fifteenth and sixteenth centuries. Later in Mexico the entire surface of free-standing stone crosses in churchyards was covered with the emblems.

The devout preoccupation with the saving death and

I its instruments was given expression in hymns saluting the wounds, lance, crown of thorns, and the rest. A modern counterpart to this would be the modern hymns "Rock of Ages" and "When I Survey the Wondrous Cross."

See separate entries as follows: Basin and Ewer; Cock; Crown of Thorns; Dice; IHC; Ladder; Lantern; Nails; Pillar and Cord; Scourges; Silver, Thirty Pieces of; Skull; Spear; Sponge; Vernicle.

Jar of Ointment

An attribute of St. Mary Magdalene, assigned to her because of the belief held throughout the Middle Ages that Mary the sister of Lazarus, the unknown sinful woman who anointed the feet of Jesus, and one of the women who brought spices to the Sepulchre were one and the same. This is her almost invariable attribute and appears as early as the thirteenth century. The Scriptural verses regarding the episode are in St. Matthew: "There came unto him a woman having an alabaster box of very precious ointment and poured it on his head, as he sat at meat . . . Wheresoever this gospel shall be preached in the whole world, there shall also this, that this woman hath done, be told for a memorial of her" (King James and Douai, *Matthew*, 26, 7 and 13).

Jesse, Root of

A symbol of Christ derived from the words of Isaiah: ". . . there shall come forth a rod out of the stem of Jesse, and a Branch shall grow out of his roots" (King James and Douai, *Isaiah*, 11, 1. In the Douai Version, the rendering differs slightly: ". . . there shall come forth a rod out of the root of Jesse, and a flower shall rise up out of his root"). This was interpreted by St. Ambrose in this manner: "The root is the family of the

Jews, the stem Mary, the flower of Mary is Christ." The antiphon known as one of the "Great O's" of the Roman Rite sung at Vespers on December 19 (by the monastic gardener in the ages when the liturgy was performed

with splendor), is addressed to Christ under this symbolical image: "O Root of Jesse, who standest for an ensign of the people, before whom kings shall keep silence, and unto Whom the Gentiles shall make their supplications: come to deliver us and tarry not."

Keys

Symbol of the spiritual powers conferred upon St. Peter
by Christ: ". . . I will give unto thee the keys of the
kingdom of heaven; and whatsoever thou shalt bind on
earth shall be bound in heaven; and whatsoever thou
shalt loose on earth shall be loosed in heaven" (King
James and Douai, *Matthew*, 16, 19). The keys are
commonly shown as one of gold and the other of silver.
A rare exception of three keys occurs on the tomb of
Otho II in the Lateran Church in Rome. The keys are
among the first distinctive attributes to be assigned to
any of the saints and anticipate by several centuries
anything like individual attributes for the other Apostles
with the exception of St. Paul's sword. Examples of St.
Peter's keys dated as early as the eighth century are
believed to be authentic, but some earlier monuments
are known to have had them added by restorers in later
times.

Knife, Sacrificial

An attribute of the Archangel (or Angel) Zadkiel who
stayed the hand of Abraham when he was about to
sacrifice Isaac. "And Abraham stretched forth his hand

K

and took the knife to slay his son. And the angel of the Lord called unto him . . . Lay not thine hand upon the lad." In the Latin of the Vulgate the weapon is a *gladius*

and is translated in the Douai Version as "sword" (King James and Douai, *Genesis*, 22, 10–12).

Ladder

Although not mentioned in the Gospel accounts of the Crucifixion, the ladder figures among the Instruments of the Passion. In representations of the Deposition, either Joseph of Arimathea or Nicodemus or both are shown on ladders removing the nails supporting the crucified body of Christ. Along with the pincers, the ladder should be among the last in a series of Passion symbols.

Lamb

This symbol of Christ, most appealing and persistent, appeared in the fourth century and was most frequently used in the fifth. Three types can be distinguished:

1. Cross-bearing, symbolizing Christ crucified, commonly with blood flowing into a chalice from a wound

in the breast; 2. Banner-bearing, signifying the Resurrection, the cross-emblazoned banner being a sign of triumph; 3. Apocalyptic, characterized by the book sealed with seven seals, symbolic of Christ as the judge at the end of the world. Scriptural texts illustrative of these three developments are ample. There are twenty-eight references to the Lamb in the Apocalypse (Revelation) alone. In prophecy, Isaiah foretold the Crucifixion. The King James Version reads, ". . . he is brought as a lamb to the slaughter . . ."; and the Douai Version, ". . . he shall be led as a sheep to the slaughter" (King James and Douai, *Isaias*, 53, 7). The paschal lamb was a decisive influence in the association of ideas finding expression in the Easter Liturgy. The hymn by St. Ambrose (A.D. 340–397), "Now at the Lamb's high royal feast" (*Ad regias Agni dapes*), remains in use.

St. John in describing the mysteries attending the opening of the sixth seal writes, ". . . hide us from the face of him that sitteth on the throne, and from the wrath of the Lamb: For the great day of his ("their" in the Douai Version) wrath is come; and who shall be able to stand" (King James, *Revelation*, 6, 16–17; Douai, *Apocalypse*, 6, 16–17).

At a synod held in Trullo, A.D. 692, legislation was passed forbidding the representation of the Lamb as a symbol of Christ. The explanation of this act was that the symbol was an image of prefiguration in the Law and that the fulfillment had been received in the Incarnation. Truth and grace required the use of the human image of Christ Who took upon Himself the sins of the world. Even though not accepted by the Western Church, this act nevertheless had an influence that led to a relegation of symbols to auxiliary or secondary importance. The lamb is one symbol which remains in use although lambs and their appeal are outside the experience of city dwellers.

As an attribute of St. John the Baptist, the symbol has undergone great degeneration. In the earliest form as at Chartres, St. John carries the cross-bearing lamb as a medallion in accord with his words: "Behold the Lamb of God, which taketh away the sin of the world" (King James and Douai, *John*, 1, 29. In the Douai Version, "Behold the Lamb of God, behold him who taketh away the sin of the world"). In the paintings of the later painters the lamb is still there but entirely naturalistic and purely an attribute.

The lamb is also an attribute of St. Agnes, assigned to her as a pun on her name. It is included in the mosaic in San Apollinare Nuovo (A.D. 493–526) in Ravenna with her representation, and is an exceptionally rare example of a distinctive attribute for a saint at so early a date.

Lamp

A symbol of Scripture as the Word of God. "Thy word is a lamp unto my feet" (King James, *Psalms*, 119, 105; Douai, *Psalms*, 118, 105). Widely diffused in the most banal stained glass, frequently accompanying an open Bible.

Lantern

An emblem of the Passion associated with the Betrayal. "Judas then, having received a band of men and officers from the chief priests and Pharisees, cometh thither with lanterns and torches and weapons" (King James and Douai, *John*, 18, 3).

Lily

Primarily a symbol of the Blessed Virgin but by extension a symbol of virginity and chastity. Combined with roses the lily was frequently an attribute of virgin saints in the Middle Ages. Chaucer was familiar with this usage:

Thou with they gerland, wrought of rose and lilie,
Thee mene I, mayde and martir, seint Cecelie.

While the white lily of Europe was regarded by the Church as emblematic of virginity, the plant called the lily of the fields, or lily of the valleys, is the anemone.

The lily is also an attribute of the Archangel Gabriel.

 Lion

This symbol of Christ has scriptural support in the apocalyptic vision recorded by St. John: ". . . Behold, the Lion of the tribe of Juda, the root of David, hath prevailed to open the book, and to loose the seven seals thereof" (King James, *Revelation*, 5, 5; Douai, *Apocalypse*, 5, 5). The writers of medieval bestiaries with their symbolic turn of mind elaborated the likeness of the lion to Christ.

Their natural history was quaint, as we view it, but they turned it to spiritual benefit by their exegesis. The nervous swishing of the lion's tail is to obliterate his footsteps. In like manner, Our Lord concealed all traces of His Godhead when He entered into the womb of the Virgin Mary and became man. It was believed that the lion slept with his eyes open. So Our Lord slept with His body in the grave, but His spirit was awake at the right hand of God. This was given further scriptural support: "Behold, he that keepeth Israel shall neither slumber nor sleep" (King James, *Psalms*, 121, 4. In the Douai Version, *Psalms*, 120, 4, "Behold he shall neither slumber nor sleep, that keepeth Israel"). It was this aspect of vigilance that dictated the use of carved stone lions to guard the portal of a church. The loud roar of the lion was explained as the means of bringing cubs to life (it was believed they were brought forth dead) by his breath. Origen says in his commentary on the Book of Genesis that this can be applied to Christ, "who was buried three days and three nights in the heart of the earth, until He had ended the sleep of death."

By more evident association of ideas, the lion is the symbol of valor, power, and courage, summed up as the cardinal virtue of Fortitude. The contrary symbol of the Devil must likewise be recognized: ". . . your adversary, the devil, as a roaring lion, walketh about, seeking whom he may devour" (King James and Douai, 1 *Peter*, 5, 8).

A lion is an attribute of St. Mark the Evangelist, but it is generally winged and distinguishes the Evangelist from St. Jerome, whose lion companion was a natural beast. In connection with St. Jerome, it is probable that we have an example of a symbol translated into an incident. In its original use, the tamed lion signified a conquered paganism now peaceful in Christian civilization. The symbol became attached to St. Jerome through a legend that he picked a thorn from the paw of a lion and that it became an affectionate pet in gratitude.

Lion, Winged

Symbol of St. Mark, following the teaching of St.

Jerome in his commentary on Ezekiel. The winged creatures are mentioned twice with slight discrepancies; "As for the likeness of their faces, they four had the face

of a man, and the face of a lion, on the right side: and they four had the face of an ox on the left side; they four also had the face of an eagle" (King James and Douai, *Ezekiel*, 1, 10. In the Douai Version: "And as for the likeness of their faces: There was the face of a man, and the face of a lion on the right side of all the four: and the face of an ox, on the left side of all four: and the face of an eagle over all the four"). Later, we read: "And every one had four faces: the first face was the face of a cherub, and the second face was the face of a man and the third of a lion, and the fourth the face of an eagle" (King James and Douai, *Ezekiel*, 10, 14). Jewish doctors had interpreted them as figures of the four Archangels, Michael, Gabriel, Raphael, and Uriel; and later as the four prophets, Isaiah, Jeremiah, Ezekiel, and Daniel. Christians transferred the emblem to the Evangelists, and there are written allusions to this as early as the second century. The visual symbols appear in the fifth century.

The traditional explanation of the attribution of the lion to St. Mark is because he wrote of the royal dignity of Christ and began his Gospel with an account of St. John the Baptist: "The voice of one crying in the wilderness . . ." (King James and Douai, *Mark*, 1, 3. The Douai Version uses "desert" in place of "wilderness").

An added reason was that St. Mark was considered the historian of the Resurrection of which, among other things, the lion was symbol.

Lyre

A symbol of pagan origin signifying concord, which was given Christian meaning along with the legend of Orpheus in the art of the catacombs. The early Fathers saw in Orpheus a suggestion of the Good Shepherd. Clement of Alexandria approved of the lyre as a device for a ring worn by Christians. Commenting on the story of Orpheus and Eurydice, he wrote "Behold the might of the New Song! It has made men out of stones, men out of beasts. Those that were as dead, not being partakers of the true life, have come to life again, simply by being hearers of this song."

Man, Winged

Symbol of St. Matthew, assigned to him in his role as Evangelist because his Gospel opens with the human genealogy of Christ, and His humanity is stressed throughout. Adam of St. Victor wrote:

> *Formam viri dant Matthaeo,*
> *Quia scripsit sic de Deo*
> *Sicut descendit ab eo*
> *Quem plasmavit homine*

> The figure of a man is given Matthew
> Because it was thus he wrote of God
> Who indeed was from Him
> Who formed man.

By the end of the Middle Ages there was little of an apocalyptic character left in representations of St. Matthew and he was shown accompanied by an angel of the current style. The four Evangelists in the sixteenth century pendatives of the Church of Santiago, Tlal-telolco, Mexico City, are an impressive contrast to later softness. Indian artists modeled them in clay in heroic size. Each rides astride a mystical beast, just as at Chartres they ride on the shoulders of the four Major Prophets.

Symbol of the Eucharist. This was used on the fifth century doors of St. Sabina in Rome in a scheme of parallelism not invented by the artist but following

tradition. "Our fathers did eat manna in the desert; as it is written, He gave them bread from heaven to eat . . . And Jesus said unto them, I am the bread of life . . ." (King James and Douai, *John*, 6, 31 and 35).

Mirror

This symbol of the Virgin is intended to set forth her nature as a reflection of God. In the Douai Version (*Wisdom*, 7, 26), we read: "For she is the brightness of eternal light, and the unspotted mirror of God's majesty, and the image of his goodness." In the Apocrypha, the passage runs: "For she is the brightness of the everlasting light, the unspotted mirror of the power of God, and the image of his goodness" (*The Wisdom of Solomon*, 7, 26). The Litany of Loreto retains the title "Mirror of Justice." During the sixteenth century, the symbol was commonly labeled *speculum sine macula* (mirror without spot).

The vessel devised during the Middle Ages for making the Eucharistic Host visible to the faithful for their veneration was used during the seventeenth and

eighteenth centuries as a symbol of the Eucharist. Countless examples are to be seen in Mexico and other Latin American countries.

The monstrance is also an attribute of St. Clare (A.D. 1194–1253). On one occasion she repelled Saracens who would have attacked her convent by appearing in a window with a monstrance in her hand.

Moon, Crescent

This symbol of the Blessed Virgin is found first in paintings intended to present the theme of the Immaculate Conception. These became popular in the early fifteenth century and incorporated imagery (as if it were heraldry) from both the Old and New Testament. "Who is she that looketh forth as the morning, fair as the moon . . ." (King James, *The Song of Solomon*, 6, 10); "Who is she that cometh forth as the morning rising, fair as the moon . . ." (Douai, *Canticle of Canticles*, 6, 9). In the Apocalypse of St. John, we find:

M

"And a great sign appeared in heaven: A woman clothed with the sun, and the moon under her feet . . ." (Douai, *Apocalypse*, 12, 1. In the King James Version, *Revelation*, 12, 1, "And there appeared a great wonder in heaven; a woman clothed with the sun, and the moon under her feet . . ."). After the battle of Lepanto, A.D. 1571, the moon under the feet of the Blessed Virgin was given the additional interpretation of the Turks subjected by the Christians, the victory of the Cross over the crescent.

Nails

The nails used in crucifying Christ will be found in every series of Passion symbols. They are not mentioned in the Gospel accounts of the Crucifixion, but their use is confirmed by the statement of St. Thomas after the Resurrection: "Except I shall see in his hands the print of the nails, and put my finger into the print of the nails, and thrust my hand into his side, I will not believe" (King James and Douai, *John*, 20, 25).

In all early representations of the Crucifixion four nails are shown, since the feet are side by side and fixed each with an individual nail. At the beginning of the thirteenth century a new convention arose of showing the crossed feet fixed with a single nail. Three nails are usual as a Passion symbol and are sometimes included with the crown of thorns.

Olive Branch

Universally accepted as a symbol of peace. The Greeks
considered the olive tree sacred to Athena, Goddess of
Wisdom, and a symbol of peace. The olive branch took
on an added significance of reconciliation between God
and man because of its use as a sign by Noah's dove
after the Deluge (see *Genesis*, 8, 11).

Orante (or Orans)

Symbol of Faith, the faith of the Church, or simply the
Church. The attitude of prayer indicated by the up-
raised arms has been interpreted by some as prayer by
those deceased for those who survive, and many such
representations are to be seen in the Roman catacombs.
Frequently the symbol is found on vessels where there
can be no association with a particular person. More

complex groupings are also found. An Orante with male figures on either side is most certainly the Church. When shown between two lions, deliverance from death is symbolized.

Organ

This familiar attribute of St. Cecilia is an example of a mistake repeated and elaborated until there is little chance that the truth will be as well known as the error. The *Golden Legend*, following early accounts of her martyrdom, records that on her wedding, ". . . she hearing the organs making melody sang in her heart only to God." The same words serve as an antiphon in the Breviary with the words "in her heart" omitted so that it is implied that she delighted in singing while accompanying herself on the organ. It should be remembered that the organ she heard was not the pipe organ known to us but something akin to the calliope, with associations for early Christians of the Roman circus and public spectacles, and that it would be more reasonable for her to trample such musical instruments under foot than to play them. Her role as organist became popular in the sixteenth century, and Raphael's painting of her helped to establish her as a favored subject for a window in a choir gallery.

Ox, Winged

Symbol of St. Luke the Evangelist. Irenaeus is credited with having assigned this mysterious creature, described by both Ezekiel and St. John, to St. Luke. The first important work of art in which the apocalyptic figures appear is the apse mosaic of St. Pudentiana in Rome at the end of the fourth or early in the fifth century. Early

writers did not agree as to which creatures signified the various Evangelists, but since the time of St. Jerome and St. Augustine the usage has been fairly constant. The ox as an animal of sacrifice was deemed appropriate for St. Luke, who emphasizes the atonement made by Christ's sufferings and death.

Palette

This attribute of St. Luke is without support in legend earlier than the tenth century. A rough drawing in the catacombs inscribed as "one of seven painted by Luca" confirmed a legend fostered by Greek painters. Most of the paintings of the Virgin attributed to St. Luke would seem to be of Greek workmanship. This charming legend was the source of some delightful late Gothic paintings showing the Virgin posing for him while he paints her portrait. Guilds of artists and schools of art have taken him without question as their patron.

Palm

Symbol of victory in the pagan world and used by Christians with the same meaning. When it appears in the catacombs it is invariably considered as a sign of a martyr's grave. In later murals and mosaics it may merely bear its original significance of victory and triumph. "After this I beheld, and, lo, a great multitude, which no man could number, of all nations, and kindreds, and people, and tongues, stood before the throne, and before the Lamb, clothed with white robes, and palms in their hands . . ." (King James, *Revelation*, 7, 9; Douai Version, *Apocalypse*, 7, 9, with slight verbal changes).

Peacock

Symbol of immortality. In the imperial days of Rome, Juno's sacred bird, the peacock, had become the emblem of the empresses. Since empresses became deities after death, the representation of the peacock became associated with release from earthly life and immortality. The pagans used the symbol not only on the tombs of the apotheosized but also on funeral lamps. Christians accepted the symbol and gave added meaning by such devices as the representation of peacocks drinking from the sacramental chalice. The bird was given even more power as a symbol of immortality by the belief that its flesh was not subject to putrefaction after death. The writers of the bestiaries found other meanings, such as the comparison of its cry in the night to the Christian who is in fear of losing grace in the darkness of life. To the modern man the accepted symbolical meaning is pride and vanity.

Pelican in her piety

This is the heraldic term for the figure of a pelican tearing open her breast (so it was thought) to feed her young. The bird standing over her young in their nest and nourishing them with her own blood is a symbol of

Christ on the Cross from whose wounded side blood and water flowed. The origin of this comparison is found in *Psalms*, 102, 6, of the King James Bible: "I am like a pelican of the wilderness." This is Verse 7 of Psalm 101 in the Douai Version: "I am become like to a pelican of the wilderness . . ." St. Augustine, commenting on this verse, wrote: "The males of these birds are wont to kill their young by blows of their beaks, and then to bewail their death for the space of three days. At length however the female inflicts a severe wound on herself and letting her blood flow over the dead young ones, brings them to life again." The excessive devotion of the pelican to its young was described by the medieval writers of bestiaries. They saw it as typifying the love of Christ in Redemption and, by association of ideas, the Eucharist. St. Thomas Aquinas used the image in his hymn *Adoro te*. "*Pie pellicane, Jesu Domine, Me immundum munda tuo sanguine*. (Pelican of mercy, Jesu Lord and God, Cleanse me, wretched sinner, in thy precious Blood)." In the art of the Middle Ages it was exclusively connected with the Crucifixion and was used as an ornament on Crosses. It came into general use with Eucharistic implications after the vision of St. Gertrude who saw Christ in this form feeding mankind.

P

Phoenix

Symbol of the Resurrection of Christ. This fabulous bird was described in the bestiaries as being native to Arabia. It was thought to reach an age of as much as five hundred years. When it foresaw its end, it was believed to build a funeral pyre and set fire to it by flapping its wings. A small worm was left among the ashes, which developed into a bird in three days. There are variations in the descriptions, but in this form the analogy with the Resurrection is clear. It appeared on Roman cinerary urns and was an acceptable symbol to Constantine, who used it on coins during his reign.

Pillar and Cord

In later Gothic times the realism in depicting the scourging of Christ ("Then Pilate therefore took Jesus and scourged him." King James and Douai, *John*, 19, 1) gave much importance to the pillar to which He was bound while being beaten. The column venerated in Jerusalem as having been the one to which Jesus was bound is mentioned as early as the fourth century. A drum of porphyry said to be a part of it was taken to Rome under Pope Honorius III (A.D. 1216–1227). Crossed scourges are frequently included with this symbol.

Pomegranate

A symbol of royalty; as such it is frequently accepted as a symbol of Christ. The pointed terminal is treated as a heraldic crown, hence the association with royalty. When designed to appear bursting with its seeds showing, it is intended as a symbol of the Resurrection, akin to the open tomb. It was an admirable decorative device for powdering throughout backgrounds and was used by glass painters in the fourteenth century and later in simulation of Italian brocades.

Ring

An attribute of St. Edward the Confessor who, according to legend, gave his ring as an alms to St. John the Baptist who appeared to him as a poor beggar. Also an attribute of St. Catherine of Siena, signifying her mystical marriage.

Rivers, Four, of Paradise

From early Christian times, accepted as a symbol of the four Evangelists. An eloquent form of the symbol depicts the rivers as flowing from a mount on which the Lamb of God stands. "And a river went out of Eden to water the garden; and from thence it was parted, and became into four heads" (King James and Douai, *Genesis*, 2, 10. The Douai Version reads: "And a river went out of the place of pleasure to water paradise, which from thence is divided into four heads"). The effect of the Gospels as preached by the four Evangelists is likened to that of rivers spreading throughout the world. Later writers found affinities between the individual Evangelists and the streams. According to Pope Innocent III (died A.D. 1216), Pison (Phison) is John, Gihon (Gehon) is Matthew, Tigris is Mark, and Euphrates is Luke.

Robe, Seamless

Symbol of the Passion frequently depicted with three dice superimposed heraldically. "The soldiers therefore when they had crucified him, took his garments (and they made four parts, to every soldier a part), and also his coat. Now the coat was without seam woven from the top throughout. They said then one to another: Let us not cut, but let us cast lots for it, whose it shall be; that the scripture might be fulfilled, saying: They have parted my garments among them, and upon my vesture they have cast lots" (King James and Douai, *John*, 19, 23–24. In the King James Version, the wording of the passage differs slightly).

Rod, Flowering

An attribute of St. Joseph, foster-father of Our Lord.

Legendary sources for the incidents in the life of St. Joseph are sometimes dated as early as the fourth century, but it was not until the fifteenth that his feast was given liturgical celebration in many parts of Europe. St. Teresa of Avila (died A.D. 1582) is credited with having caused great increase in devotion to him. Ancient as the story of the flowering rod may be, it persists as an almost invariable stalk of lilies in popular representations of St. Joseph.

According to the legend, the priest Zacharias was instructed by an angel to call all the widowers together and to place their rods in the temple overnight. The following morning, Joseph's rod was found to have flowered, and he was told to take the Virgin and to keep her for the Lord. In paintings of the subject, the rejected suitors are shown breaking their rods with expressions of envy and disgust.

Rose

Symbol of the Blessed Virgin; it figures in the Litany of Loreto as the Mystical Rose. Popular devotion connected the Virgin with many plants and flowers in the Middle Ages. These associations can still be traced by the inclusion of "Lady" in their present-day names, e.g., "Lady's Slipper," "Lady's Smock," and the like. Religious poets and theologians explored the flower world for images and symbols of the Blessed Mother. In the five petals of the wild rose were seen the five joys of Mary, and a reminder of the five letters in Maria. Like many of the symbols of the Virgin, these found warrant in verses of Scripture. "I was exalted like a palm tree in Cades ("En-gaddi" in the King James

Apocrypha), and as a rose plant in Jericho" (Douai, *Ecclesiasticus*, 24, 18). In Douai, *Ecclesiasticus*, 39, 17, we read: "Hear me, ye divine offspring, and bud forth as the rose planted by the brooks of waters." The King James Apocrypha (*Ecclesiasticus*, 39, 13) translates the passage: "Hearken unto me, ye holy children, and bud forth as a rose growing by the brook of the field."

The widespread popularity of the devotion of the Rosary has been influential in perpetuation of this symbol, and has established a symbolical use of white roses for the Joyful Mysteries, red roses for the Sorrowful, and yellow or golden for the Glorious.

Saw

Scripture reports nothing of St. Simon the Apostle beyond the fact that Our Lord called him and that he was present on Pentecost. He is identified in *Matthew*, 10, 4, as Simon the "Canaanite" ("Cananean" in the Douai Version). To avoid confusion with Simon Peter he is also called Simon Zelotes (King James and Douai, *Acts*, 1, 13). With so little to inspire graphic representations, traditional legends have been drawn upon with confusing results. The instrument of his martyrdom has been described as a saw and as a falchion. The same attributes are assigned to his fellow Apostle St. Jude, whose feast is celebrated with his in the Western Church on October 28. When one is represented with a saw, the other receives a falchion, and vice versa. Fish, ships, and oars are additional attributes for them, without justification other than the medieval supposition that they were cousins of the sons of Zebedee and were therefore fishermen.

In late medieval art the prophet Isaiah was given a saw as an attribute, since it was thought to have been the instrument of his death.

Scales

Attribute of St. Michael the Archangel signifying his office as conductor of the souls of the dead to judgment. Ancient Egyptian and Indian belief had been that virtues and vices would hang in a balance at judgment, and the metaphor was popular in early Christian writing.

St. John Chrysostom wrote: "In that day our actions, our words, our thoughts will be placed in the scales, and the dip of the balance on either side will carry with it the irrevocable sentence." The contrast of good and bad was achieved variously: a figure kneeling in prayer opposed to toads and a gruesome head, the Agnus Dei and an obvious reprobate, the lamp of vigilance and a hideous figure. St. Michael's attribute established him as the patron of all who work with scales, such as bakers and druggists.

Scales are likewise an attribute of the choir of angels called Thrones. A source for the attribution is: "For thou hast maintained my right and my cause; thou satest in the throne judging right" (King James, *Psalms*, 9, 4). The Douai Version numbers this Verse 5 and renders it: "For thou hast maintained my judgment and my cause: thou hast sat on the throne, who judgest justice."

Scourges

"Then released he Barabbas unto them: and when he had scourged Jesus, he delivered him to be crucified"

(King James, *Matthew*, 27, 26). The same chapter and verse in the Douai Version reads: "Then he released to them Barabbas: and having scourged Jesus, delivered him unto them to be crucified." The final episode of the Flagellation is symbolized by scourges. These usually have several tails of knotted cord and are crossed saltire, or are displayed with the pillar to which Christ was tied.

Scroll

This early form of manuscript was not supplanted by the codex until the fourth century. Hence it was used as the symbol of wisdom and was the earliest attribute of the Apostles. It was carried by St. Peter for centuries before the keys became his symbol, and the same is true for St. Paul whose sword appeared about the tenth century. While it is strictly an anachronism to depict Christ with a book, common usage has established it, and the scroll would appear to this generation as stuffy antiquarianism. The scroll is frequently used as a symbol for Elias where the tablets of the Law are used for Moses in symbolical representations of the Transfiguration.

Seat of Wisdom

Symbol of the Blessed Virgin, based on a title in the

Litany of Loreto. This title of Our Lady is found in the writings of St. Anselm in the eleventh century and of St. Bernard in the twelfth.

Serpent

Symbol of evil and particularly of Satan who tempted Eve in this form. "Now the serpent was more subtil than any beast of the field which the Lord God had made. And he said unto the woman, Yea, hath God said, Ye shall not eat of every tree of the garden?" (King James and Douai, *Genesis*, 3, 1. In the Douai Version, the serpent says, "Why hath God commanded you, that you should not eat of every tree of paradise?") Among writers who see the Virgin as a new Eve, the serpent figures among her symbols as a fulfillment of the prophecy: "I will put enmity between thee and the woman, and between thy seed and her seed; it shall bruise thy head, and thou shalt bruise his heel" (King James and Douai, *Genesis*, 3, 15. In the Douai Version this reads: "I will put enmities between thee and the woman, and thy seed and her seed: she shall crush thy head, and thou shalt lie in wait for her heel").

The pious belief was once prevalent that all snakes remained in their holes on August 15, the feast of the Assumption of the Blessed Virgin. A serpent with an apple in its mouth, encircling the globe, has become a much used symbol of the Immaculate Conception.

Serpent, Brazen

Symbol of Christ crucified. "And as Moses lifted up the serpent in the wilderness, even so must the Son of man

be lifted up" (King James and Douai, *John*, 3, 14).
While this might seem to refer to the Ascension as
much as the Crucifixion, it was the latter event which

was preferred in the Middle Ages. St. Augustine in
preaching on this passage from St. John said, "What is
the serpent lifted up? The death of the Lord on the cross.
For as death came by the serpent, it was figured by the
image of a serpent." Although this symbol is mentioned
in the Gospel, it does not appear in the earliest art. It
was one of the pictures St. Benedict Biscop obtained in
Rome for the church at Jarrow in A.D. 685. By the
thirteenth century it was a standard symbol accompanying the Crucifixion.

Shamrock

Symbol of the Trinity used by St. Patrick, according to
legend, to demonstrate that mystery to Leoghaire, Chief
of Chiefs in Ireland. It so happened that the Feast of
Tara fell at the same time as the Christian Easter. All
fires were quenched throughout the country. For the
infringement of this custom, death was the penalty. St.
Patrick ordered the Paschal fire kindled. When Leoghaire went with his men to apprehend the violator of the
law, he was treated with a sermon from St. Patrick in

the course of which the saint picked a shamrock and used it as a symbol of the triune God.

Sheep, Twelve

Symbol of the Twelve Apostles. The usual form of representation is a line of sheep with Christ as the Good Shepherd in the center, or as the Lamb of God with

cruciform halo standing on a mound from which flow the four rivers of paradise. At the extremities the gates of Jerusalem and Bethlehem sometimes appear. The apsidal mosaics in the churches of SS. Cosmas and Damian, St. Cecilia, St. Clement, and St. Praxedes in Rome are examples of this treatment. In a later variation of this theme the Apostles are men accompanied by sheep.

Shell, Scallop

Symbol of the Apostle St. James the Greater. This, like his distinctive pilgrim garb, has nothing to do with any event in his life. It is due solely to the popularity of his shrine at Compostela in Spain. As a pilgrim's goal this shrine was second only to Rome, and during the thirteenth century it became the custom to depict St.

James as a pilgrim with his staff from which a gourd for water or a wallet is suspended. The shell is usually affixed to his shoulder or hat and is not invariably a scallop in medieval art. There are representations in which the shell is a cockle or whelk. The most reasonable explanation of the scallop shell is that it is plentiful on the coast of Galicia and provided a handy spoon or cup, and was therefore carried away by pilgrims as a souvenir.

The shell is also a symbol of Baptism. The manner of representing the Baptism of Christ has always followed the current mode of administering the Sacrament. In the earliest examples, the water surrounds the body of Christ to suggest the depth of water required for immersion. This convention persisted until the end of the twelfth century, when Baptism by poured water began to be represented. Since that time the shell has been the most common container of the water in Italian paintings, while a small jug was favored by German and Flemish painters.

Shepherd, Good

"I am the good shepherd. The good shepherd giveth his life for his sheep" (King James and Douai, *John*, 10, 11). This was the favorite symbolical representation of Christ during the early centuries of the Church. It is found on the walls of the catacombs, on sarcophagi, and in the mosaics of ancient Italian churches. This appealing symbol took two forms—the Good Shepherd carrying a sheep on his shoulders, or keeping watch with his flock. In some representations in the catacombs the shepherd carries musical pipes like Pan. This is an adaptation from pagan sources and would have been useful in hiding the meaning from the uninitiated. This symbol passed out of use after the eleventh century and did not reappear until the sixteenth. For many people the immediate association would be derived from the first verse of the King James Version of the Twenty-third Psalm: "The Lord is my shepherd; I shall not want." The Douai Version numbers this the Twenty-second Psalm and omits the shepherd imagery: "The Lord ruleth me: and I shall want nothing."

No representation of Christ was more popular than Plockhorst's "Good Shepherd" during the art-glass era at the turn of this century, when it was a practice of commercial-minded glassmen to keep it in stock in several sizes. All that was needed to fit any window opening was a border to fill it out. Fresh inspiration is needed to revitalize this symbol.

Ship

Symbol of the Church, sometimes represented with Christ or St. Peter as helmsman. St. Hippolytus in the third century wrote: "The world is a sea, in which the Church, like a ship, is beaten by the waves, but not submerged." It was among the devices approved by Clement of Alexandria for rings worn by Christians. The symbolism lingers in the architectural term of "nave" to describe the main body of the church reserved for the congregation.

During the late Middle Ages a more elaborate symbolism was developed with both Church and Synagogue personified and contrasted. The Church was arrayed in regal robes, wearing a crown and carrying a chalice, crozier, and the Cross or a banner. In contrast the Synagogue wore a torn mantle (or one which appeared to be slipping from her shoulders); her eyes were covered with a veil, and she held the Tablets of the Law and a broken staff.

A ship is assigned to the Apostle Jude as an attribute on the assumption that he was a fisherman.

Silver, thirty pieces of

"And (Judas) said unto them, What will ye give me, and I will deliver him unto you? And they covenanted with him for thirty pieces of silver" (King James and Douai, *Matthew*, 26, 15. The Douai Version reads: "But they appointed him thirty pieces of silver"). This symbol of the Betrayal is properly the first in any series of Passion instruments. The pieces of silver are sometimes shown falling from a bag or are arranged circular-wise around it.

The circumstance of the calling of St. Matthew to be an Apostle has provided him with the distinctive emblem of a purse or money bag. "And as Jesus passed forth from thence, he saw a man sitting at the receipt of custom; and he said unto him, Follow me. And he arose, and followed him" (King James and Douai, *Matthew*, 9, 9). In England during the fifteenth century the attribute was often a sturdy cash-box. The attribute of St. Matthew was a long time in becoming fixed. The *Golden Legend* describes his death as having been caused by a sword, but in early representations he quite often carries a halberd or spear.

Skull

Frequently introduced at the foot of the Cross in representations of the Crucifixion. "And he bearing his cross went forth into a place called the place of a skull, which is called in the Hebrew Golgotha . . ." (King James and Douai, *John*, 19, 17. The Latin word for skull is *calvaria*, hence the Douai translation based on the Vulgate reads: ". . . he went forth to the place which is called Calvary, but in Hebrew Golgotha"). It is a tradition of the Eastern Church that the Crucifixion took place over the spot where Adam was buried—the Second Adam undoing the work of the first.

As an emblem of death, the skull was carved on innumerable tombstones throughout New England. Such an emphasis on the dissolution of the body can scarcely qualify as Christian, and present law in the Roman Church forbids the use of skull and crossed tibia on palls and vestments.

This symbol is also found as an attribute for ascetic saints such as Jerome. In this connection it infers contemplation on man's end as seen in the light of eternity and not merely morbidity.

Spear

"But one of the soldiers with a spear opened his side: and immediately there came out blood and water" (King James and Douai, *John*, 19, 34). For decorative effect the spear is usually displayed with the sponge on a reed. Properly these belong among Instruments of the

Passion most intimately connected with the Crucifixion. Although in various parts of the world there are several relics purporting to be the lance which opened the side of Christ, none has credible authentication. A liturgical office in honor of the Spear and Nails was instituted in 1354.

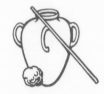

Sponge

"Now there was set a vessel full of vinegar: and they filled a sponge with vinegar, and put it upon hyssop, and put it to his mouth" (King James and Douai, *John*, 19, 29). As described above, the sponge is usually combined with the spear saltire-wise. The vat of vinegar (common dry wine of the soldiers) sometimes appears as a separate item in extended series of Passion instruments.

Square, Carpenter's

The usual symbol of St. Thomas the Apostle, a fisherman whose association with building and his patronage of architects and builders is owing to an apocryphal legend. The *Golden Legend* recounts the story in this way: "Thomas having been told by the Lord that he would go to India was engaged as an architect for Gondofer, the king of India at the time. He was able to draw plans in the Roman style for the King who after having entrusted him with large sums of money set out

93

for distant parts of his kingdom. Thomas promptly distributed the money to the poor and gave himself up to preaching. When the King returned after two years Thomas was flogged and thrown into prison to await death by being burned alive. The course of justice was upset by an opportune vision the King had of his brother who had recently died. He reported the splendor of the heavenly mansion St. Thomas had caused to be prepared for the King and his desire to have it for himself. The King was reluctant to part with his heavenly property unseen and begged St. Thomas to prepare a like place for his brother. St. Thomas took the opportunity to preach a sermon on the right use of riches."

Staff

This common support used while walking great distances is the attribute used to signify pilgrimage. It was so familiar a sight in earlier ages that it was an attribute of St. Peter, along with a Cross, before keys became his identifying symbol. Souls appearing for judgment are sometimes depicted with a staff, and even Our Lord has been represented with it to suggest that the Incarnation was a long pilgrimage. Even those who have never used a walking stick understand the words of the Psalmist, "Thy rod and thy staff they comfort me." St. James the Great invariably carries a staff, and St. Christopher, being a giant, used a tree for his support.

Staff and Gourd

Attributes of St. Raphael the Archangel, the guardian of Tobias. Pilgrim saints may exhibit the same objects. St. Raphael is easily identified when, in addition to his staff and gourd, he carries a fish and he and his companion are followed by a dog.

Stag

Symbol of the faithful Christian longing for God, or in earlier centuries the catechumen desiring Baptism. It finds origin in the poetical image in *Psalms* (King James,

42, 1): "As the hart panteth after the waterbrooks, so panteth my soul after thee, O God." The Psalm is the Forty-first in the Douai Version and reads: "As the hart panteth after the fountains of water; so my soul panteth after thee, O God." The stag was a favored decoration in baptisteries in the fourth century, where for the sake of symmetry stags were represented in pairs (contrary to the strict sense of the Psalm), drinking from the waters of paradise. The writers of the bestiaries found elaborate symbolism in the habits of the stag.

The stag is likewise the attribute of St. Eustace and St. Hubert, where it is considered as an image of Christ the Savior.

Star

Symbol of the Epiphany, and not of the Nativity as Christmas decorations and cards would lead us to believe. ". . . and behold, the star, which they had seen in the east went before them until it came and stood over where the child was" (King James and Douai, *Matthew*, 2, 9).

The star is also a symbol of Christ: "I am the root and stock of David, the bright and morning star" (Douai, *Apocalypse*, 22, 16; King James, *Revelation*, 22,

16). This imagery is also found in the Old Testament: ". . . there shall come a Star out of Jacob, and a Sceptre shall rise out of Israel . . ." (King James and Douai, *Numbers*, 24, 17. The Douai Version reads: "A star shall rise out of Jacob and a sceptre shall spring up from Israel . . ."). In a second century fresco in the catacombs, Balaam is shown pointing to the Star of the Epiphany as if in confirmation of his prophecy.

The star is likewise a symbol of the Blessed Virgin. Her bearing of Christ without loss of her virginity is seen as similar to stars sending out their light without loss of brightness. The hymn *Ave maris stella*, thought to be by Venantius Fortunatus (sixth century), has helped to make this symbol popular. In paintings of the Blessed Virgin in the Eastern tradition, her mantle is decorated with three stars, one on each shoulder and one on the veil. These are seen as symbolical of her virginity, before, during, and after the bearing of Our Lord. The crown of twelve stars sometimes seen is drawn from the description of the woman clothed with the sun: "And a great sign appeared in heaven: a woman clothed with the sun, and the moon under her feet, and on her head a crown of twelve stars . . .") King James, *Revelation*; *Apocalypse* in Douai; 12, 1). This apocalyptic description has been drawn on by painters attempting to depict the mystery of the Immaculate Conception.

The glory behind Christ in icons sometimes takes the form of an eight-pointed star. This is an allusion to the teaching that the day on which Christ rose was the eighth of creation, a beginning of days outside of time and a symbol of eternity.

A star in his halo is an attribute of St. Dominic. St. Nicholas of Tolentino is represented with a star on the breast of his black garb (not to be confused with St. Thomas Aquinas who has the sun on his breast and wears a black and white habit).

Sword

A symbol of spiritual armament appropriate to St. Paul and attributed to him in the tenth century because of his teaching: "And take unto you the helmet of salvation and the sword of the Spirit, which is the word of God" (King James and Douai, *Ephesians*, 6, 17). It also refers to his death as a martyr. St. Paul's words regarding the sword of the spirit were seen by medieval writers as being applicable to Fortitude, and the sword became the symbol of that virtue in the thirteenth century.

Sword, Flaming

The attribute of Jophiel, the guardian of the tree of knowledge, who drove Adam and Eve from the garden of Eden. "Therefore the Lord God sent him forth from the garden of Eden, to till the ground from whence he was taken. So he drove out the man: and he placed at the east of the garden of Eden cherubim, and a flaming sword which turned every way, to keep the way of the tree of life" (King James and Douai, *Genesis*, 3, 23–24. The reading in the Douai Version is: "And the Lord

God sent him out of the paradise of pleasure, to till the earth from which he was taken. And he cast out Adam; and placed before the paradise of pleasure Cherubims, and a flaming sword, turning every way, to keep the way of the tree of life"). In the Western Church Jophiel is not recognized as an Archangel. Michael, Gabriel, and Raphael alone find a place in the Liturgy by name. Jophiel and others from apocryphal and legendary sources have appeared in art but have no official standing in Christian teaching.

Sword and Scales

Symbols of Justice and commonly attributes of St. Michael. The sword recalls his battle with Lucifer, and the scales represent his position as the Lord of Souls at judgment.

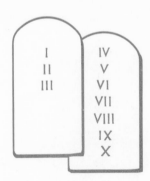

Tablets of the
Ten Commandments

The tablets figure as an attribute of the Old Dispensation (the Synagogue) compared with the New (the Church). The Commandments are not individually numbered in the Bible, and the later division and numbering of the clauses has led to differences in representation. "And Moses turned, and went down from the mount, and the two tables of the testimony were in his hand: the tables were written on both their sides; on the one side and on the other were they written" (King James and Douai, *Exodus*, 32, 15. The translation in the Douai Version is more direct: "And Moses returned from the mount, carrying the two tables of the testimony in his hand, written on both sides"). The two tablets are always used. Since writing on both sides as described in the Bible is impractical, the Commandments (or numerals standing for them) are shown in various groupings. The Jewish practice of five on each table is ancient and is attested by Josephus. Catholics and Lutherans follow the division adopted by St. Augustine, in which three are placed on the first table and seven on the second. This exhibits the symbolical numbers three and seven, with the total of ten. The division accepted by the Reformed churches at the Reformation is in groups of four and six.

Throne

Symbol of the majesty of Christ, appearing in mosaic decoration as early as the fifth century. Its scriptural support is found in such verses as "But the Lord shall

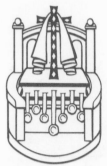

endure for ever: he hath prepared his throne for judgment" (King James, *Psalms*, 9, 7; *Psalms*, 9, 8 in the Douai Version). The accessories of the throne usually strengthen the thought of Christ coming as judge—the jeweled Cross occupying the throne, the Book with Seven Seals, the royal mantle, or the dove hovering above.

Tower of David (and of Ivory)

Poetical images from the fourth and seventh chapters of the Song of Solomon (the Canticle of Canticles in the Douai Version). Although the phrases were used as early as the twelfth century by Honorius of Autun in praise of the Virgin and they are included among the invocations in the Litany of Loreto, they are not intended in praise of physical beauty. They mean rather that the Blessed Mother is the glory of the House of David and is the model of inviolable purity. These symbols figure in series from the Litany and are frequently used surrounding the figure of the Virgin in an attempt to give visual expression to the doctrine of the Immaculate Conception.

Tree of Life

"And out of the ground made the Lord God to grow every tree that is pleasant to the sight and good for food; the tree of life also in the midst of the garden, and the tree of knowledge of good and evil" (King James and Douai, *Genesis*, 2, 9. The Douai Version says, "And the Lord God brought forth of the ground all manner of trees, fair to behold, and pleasant to eat of: the tree of life also in the midst of paradise: and the tree of knowledge of good and evil"). The tree has been an ever present witness to the change of seasons with its pattern of hope, fulfillment, and resurrection after decline. The Christmas tree and the May Pole are two adaptations from the pagan world of myth and folklore which are well known to modern man. In Christian symbolism the Cross has been seen as the true Tree of Life and the tree in the garden of Eden a prefiguration of it. Those who eat of the tree in the heavenly Jerusalem do so as a result of the redemption wrought on the Cross. The medieval turn of thought is exemplified in the hymn sung during the veneration of the Cross on Good Friday in the Roman Rite:

Eating of the tree forbidden,
Man had sunk in Satan's snare,
When his pitying Creator
Did this second tree prepare
Destined many ages later,
That first evil to repair.

Triangle, Equilateral

Symbol of the Trinity. The Athanasian Creed sums up the doctrine of the Trinity thus: ". . . we worship one God in Trinity, and Trinity in unity; neither confounding the Persons, nor dividing the substance. For

there is one Person of the Father, another of the Son, another of the Holy Ghost. But the Godhead of the Father, and of the Son, and of the Holy Ghost is but one, the glory equal, and the majesty coeternal." Attempts to express this profound mystery in symbols display a great diversity. The early Christians used the Hand for God the Father, the Cross or Lamb for God the Son, and a Dove for God the Holy Ghost. Examples from this period are to be seen in the churches of SS. Cosmas and Damian and St. Praxedes in Rome. This treatment was used in Rome as late as the thirteenth and fourteenth centuries. A second phase introduced anthropomorphic features, with the three Persons represented in human form of identical or varied age. A third stage was reached in attempts to make a coherence of three heads on one body or three faces on one head. This was forbidden by Pope Urban VIII in A.D. 1628.

During the Middle Ages geometrical symbols were developed, emphasizing both unity and triplicity. During the thirteenth century three interlinked circles were used with two Latin words *Unitas* (unity) and *Trinitas* (trinity). In the fifteenth century an even more explicit symbol became popular. The ends of a triangle were labeled *Pater* (Father), *Filius* (Son), and *Spiritus* (Spirit). These were connected with the phrase *non est* (is not). All three were connected with the word *Deus* (God) in the center with the word *est* (is).

The feast of the Most Holy Trinity was extended to the Universal Church in A.D. 1334.

Unicorn

A symbol of both Christ and chastity. This legendary creature was supposed to be by nature exceedingly swift. No hunter could capture it by skill. The necessary ruse was to have a virgin wait for it near its shelter. It became a simple matter to capture or kill it when it grew gentle at sight of her and placed its head in her lap. Just so was Christ, born of a virgin mother, considered imaginatively as a spiritual unicorn. The Council of Trent, in view of the advance in scientific knowledge at the time, forbade the use of the unicorn as a symbol of the Incarnation.

Although it was accepted as a symbol of chastity, the unicorn is not properly used as a symbol of the Virgin.

Vernicle

The veil of Veronica, retaining the image of Jesus after she had wiped His face when on the way to Calvary, appears in many series of Passion symbols. The story of its origin is legendary. The name Veronica itself has been explained as a corruption of *vera icon* (true image).

Although St. Veronica figures in the Stations of the Cross, she is a late addition to that devotion. The cloth supposed to be hers in St. Peter's is reported to have lost all trace of the likeness.

Vine

The words of Christ are the origin of this eloquent symbol. "I am the vine; you are the branches. He that abideth in me, and I in him, the same beareth much fruit: for without me you can do nothing" (King James

V and Douai, *John*, 15, 5). This symbol has been used since the earliest times. In a window dated A.D. 1625 in Troyes Cathedral, the Apostles are shown occupying a vine rising from the breast of Christ.

Water

A symbol of purification by the very nature of its cleansing properties. In Scripture it is the symbol of tribulation, as in *Psalms*, 69, 1–2 (King James): "Save me, O God; for the waters are come in unto my soul. I sink in deep mire, where there is no standing: I am come into deep waters, where the floods overflow me." The same passage is translated in *Psalms*, 68, 2–3, of the Douai Version: "Save me, O God: for the waters are come in even unto my soul. I stick fast in the mire of the deep: and there is no sure standing. I am come into the depth of the sea: and a tempest hath overwhelmed me." As one of the four elements it is symbolized by a swan. A few drops of water are mingled with the wine in the Roman Mass; the water symbolizes the humanity of Christ and the wine His divinity. The water struck from the rock by Moses was seen by early Christians as a prefiguration of Baptism. As such it appears among the frescoes in the catacombs. On the sarcophagus of Junius Bassus (died A.D. 359) in the crypt of St. Peter's the figure of Moses striking the rock is not represented, but a lamb performs the miracle.

Wells, Three (or Fountains)

According to tradition, St. Paul's head struck the earth

in three places after his martyrdom, and at each a fountain appeared. These are sometimes used as a symbol of his death. The present church on the site of

St. Paul's beheading dates from A.D. 1599 and replaces an ancient one of unknown foundation. The altars in the three chapels are raised over the wells.

XP (Chi Rho)

The history of this symbol extends from its beginning as a monogram incorporating the first two letters of the name of Christ in Greek characters (ΧΡΙΣΤΟΣ) to the

Cross openly used for the first time by Christians during the fifth century. It was sometimes used in catacomb inscriptions as early as the second century, combining both Greek and Latin—"In ☧." Its use as an independent symbol cannot be proved by examples prior to the time of Constantine, whose name has been given to it because of its use on his standard, the *Labarum*. Shortly after his time, the Greek letters A and Ω were added to the monogram as an affirmation of the Divinity of Christ. On a lead coffin of the fourth century it has been found encircled with the Greek letters signifying "Jesus Son of God and Savior." The monogram implied triumph; hence it fell into oblivion after the Goths conquered Rome, being then supplanted by the Cross. In rare instances it survived and was transplanted as far as Scotland and Wales, where it was used on stone monuments.

When for some reason of design the monogrammatic form is not used and the letters stand side by side, they should read XP—not PX.

A BRIEF
ANNOTATED BIBLIOGRAPHY

Barbier de Montault, Msgr. X.
Traité d'Iconographie Chrétienne, Paris, 1900.
The entire field of Christian iconography, symbolism, and attributes of the saints in their accepted forms is presented with brief explanations. The emphasis is on *what* rather than *why*. When this is understood the book can be useful.

Bond, Francis
Dedications and Patron Saints of English Churches, London, 1914.
Brief lives are given of all the saints who were popular enough to have had churches dedicated to them during the Middle Ages. Most of the illustrations of the saints, their emblems, and symbols are from little-known English examples. One chapter is devoted to ecclesiastical symbolism.
Wood Carvings in English Churches, (Vol. I, Misericords), London, 1910.
Many real and fanciful beasts were favorite subjects for carvings under medieval choir seats. Most of the creatures were endowed with moral and symbolical values and many are retained as symbols today. As much of the lore of the bestiaries as an average person will wish for is given in this book.

Butler, Alban
Lives of the Saints (Edited, revised and supplemented by Herbert Thurston, S.J., and Donald Attwater), New York, 1956.
Based on the best authorities and critically written. This book might well be the ready reference book for the modern artist that the *Golden Legend* was for the medieval man.

Didron, A. N.
Christian Iconography (Translated from the French by E. J. Millington, and completed with additions and appendices by Margaret Stokes), London, 1886. In addition to information on western medieval usage, Byzantine variations are described and illustrated. The appendices include the text of *Biblia Pauperum*, and the Byzantine *Guide to Painting*.

Drake, Maurice and Wilfred
Saints and Their Emblems, London, 1916.
A vast compilation listing many little-known saints and their attributes. For convenience the attributes are cross-indexed. Sources and authorities are cited in a trustworthy manner, without fanciful inventions for those saints who have no distinctive attributes.

Durandus, William
The Symbolism of Churches and Church Ornaments (Translated with an introductory essay and notes by the Rev. John Mason Neale and the Rev. Benjamin Webb), London, 1893.
This will be read by the lovers of the curious rather than by those with any practical purpose. It is unlikely to prompt anything vital in religious thinking today. Its chief value seems to be in its quotability.

Jameson, Anna
Sacred and Legendary Art (Edited with additional notes by Estelle Hurll), Boston, 1896.
The History of Our Lord, 4th ed., London, 1888.
Legends of the Madonna, 6th ed., London, 1879.
Legends of the Monastic Orders, 7th ed., London, 1888.
Probably the most popular books on religious art ever published in English. They will be found in every studio of church art and in many second-hand bookshops. It is a rare point on which Mrs Jameson does not give at least a brief remark.

Lowrie, Walter
Art in the Early Church, New York, 1947.
The author is concerned more with the inner and essential meaning of early Christian art than with its changing form. Architecture, sculpture, painting, illustration and the lesser arts are all surveyed in a scholarly, lively and original manner.

Mâle, Emile
L'Art religieux du XIIe siècle en France, Paris, 1924.
L'Art religieux du XIIIe siècle en France, Paris, 1898. English translation by D. Nussey, London and New York, 1913. Reprinted under the title *The Gothic Image*. New York, 1958.
L'Art religieux de la fin du moyen âge en France, Paris, 1925. These are indispensable source books on the art and symbolism of the Middle Ages.

Reau, Louis
Iconographie de l'Art Chrétien. Tome I, *Introduction Générale*, Paris, 1955; Tome II, *Iconographie de la Bible* (in two volumes: *Ancien Testament*, Paris, 1956; *Nouveau Testament*, Paris, 1957).
A brilliant and comprehensive work. The information is logically presented, thoroughly documented and written with flashes of humor which will not always please the pious.

Roig, Juan Ferrando
Iconografía de los Santos, Barcelona, 1950.
Many little-known Spanish saints are included. The illustrations are a pleasant contrast to those in familiar English manuals because they are taken from Spanish churches, museums, and popular prints. Travelers in Mexico will find it useful for identifying saints who are rarely seen in churches north of the border.

115

Rushforth, G. McN.
Medieval Christian Imagery, Oxford, 1936.
Written with the primary intention of making the subjects of the fifteenth century stained glass in Great Malvern Priory intelligible to a present-day audience. Almost the whole of Christian iconography is covered and the development of each subject is traced from early examples to the late form seen at Malvern. As in all works of this general nature, many references to symbols and attributes are included.

Twining, Louisa
Symbols and Emblems of Early and Mediaeval Christian Art, London, 1885.
A treatise on the major symbols. Examples are carefully dated.

de Voragine, Jacobus
The Golden Legend (Translated and adapted from the Latin by Granger Ryan and Helmut Ripperger), New York, 1941.
The collection of lives of the saints that was universally used by medieval artists. It is the most available book to aid in understanding why saints were pictured as they were and why they were given their popular attributes.

White, T. H. (translator)
The Book of Beasts, New York, 1954.
A translation of a twelfth century English bestiary. Such books were intended as natural history with moral and religious lessons added for edification. They are the source of our knowledge of what symbolical meanings the medieval man read into the habits and characteristics of seen and unseen creatures.

Winzen, Damusus, O.S.B.
Symbols of Christ, New York, 1955.
Twenty symbols from the Old and New Testaments are interpreted with cosmic and Christian significance.

INDEX